In captivating conversational style, Dr. Payne raises practical questions about evangelism, then offers thoughtful biblical answers. I find especially noteworthy his treatment of the Reformed and Wesleyan-Arminian traditions, regarding the issues of divine sovereignty and human choice in election. It's an invigorating discussion, and the reader will not come away unrewarded.

ROBERT COLEMAN
Distinguished Professor of Evangelism and Discipleship
Gordon-Conwell Theological Seminary

Let me state it as simply as I can—this is an excellent book! It's clear and accessible, biblically rich and theologically informed. It will prove to be a great resource to encourage and challenge evangelism among God's people. If you find evangelism scary, read this book. It won't take away all your anxiety, but it will give you the framework and tools to at least start to calm the fear and enable you to start to see evangelism as a privilege rather than a threat.

STEVE TIMMIS
Church Planter
Co-author, *Total Church: A Radical Reshaping Around Gospel and Community*

Though the word is not used in the title, this book is actually a great book on theology as it relates to evangelism. The tough questions related to evangelism are skillfully answered, and yet the book is filled with practical material which any aspiring witness needs to know. This book will be as helpful to you as any book on evangelism. Read it and it will go a long way in helping you to do it well.

DR. ROY J. FISH
Distinguished Professor of Evangelism Emeritus
Southwestern Baptist Theological Seminary

The telling of the good news of Jesus Christ involves both timeless and timely elements. It is timeless in its unchanging truth of salvation, but it must be delivered in a timely manner to a given context and culture. J. D. Payne has given the church a readable, concisely written, and immensely practical book that brings together well both the timely and timeless. He deals in a marvelous way with both key theological concepts and practical questions believers ask.

ALVIN L. REID, PH.D.
Professor of Evangelism and Student Ministry
Bailey Smith Chair of Evangelism
Southeastern Baptist Theological Seminary

J. D. Payne's *Evangelism: A Biblical Response to Today's Questions* has provided a unique and excellent resource for anyone interested in biblical evangelism. He has gathered an amazing list of questions, answering them one-by-one with gentleness, tact, and biblical clarity. I heartily recommend *Evangelism*.

THOMAS P. JOHNSTON, PH.D.
Associate Professor of Evangelism
Midwestern Baptist Theological Seminary

Why don't believers share the Gospel more often than they do? It may be due to questions they have about evangelism that no one has ever answered for them. J. D. Payne, combining the knowledge of a scholar with the skill of a practitioner, answers thirty-three common questions that Christians have in preparing to share their faith. His answers are saturated with Scripture and pastoral wisdom. This book will help you in your witnessing—read it! It will help others as well—share it!

TIMOTHY K. BEOUGHER
Billy Graham Professor of Evangelism
The Southern Baptist Theological Seminary

EVANGELISM

A BIBLICAL RESPONSE TO TODAY'S QUESTIONS

J. D. PAYNE

Transforming lives through God's Word

Transforming lives through God's Word

Biblica provides God's Word to people through translation, publishing and Bible engagement in Africa, Asia Pacific, Europe, Latin America, Middle East, and North America. Through its worldwide reach, Biblica engages people with God's Word so that their lives are transformed through a relationship with Jesus Christ.

Biblica Publishing
We welcome your questions and comments.

1820 Jet Stream Drive, Colorado Springs, CO 80921 USA
www.Biblica.com

Evangelism
ISBN-13: 978-1-60657-009-8

Other Books by J. D. Payne

Missional House Churches: Reaching Our Communities with the Gospel

The Barnabas Factors: Eight Essential Practices of Church Planting Team Members

Discovering Church Planting: An Introduction to the Whats, Whys, and Hows of Global Church Planting

To the Sovereign Soul Winner who holds the
answers to all questions,
and to Sarah, the answer he provided when I asked.

CONTENTS

FOREWORD

Professor Payne knows what practical philosopher Plato, Protestant reformer Luther, Puritan catechist Baxter, Baptist colossus Spurgeon, and many more have also known, namely that in behavioral and relational matters, more is communicated faster and at a deeper level through the to-and-fro of dialogue than by any other means. So the reader of this book should tune in to Mark, the young Christian whom Roberto mentors in Dr. Payne's dialogues. Keep in step with Mark as he asks his questions, is taught, and learns.

One thing to note about Mark at once: he is wholly free of the spiritual infection that we might call wriggle-out-itis, which Scripture shows us going right back to the start of human sin. The essence of this infection is evading responsibility in its various forms. We see it in Adam, as he blames Eve for his eating of the forbidden fruit; we see it in Cain, as he pretends not to know what has happened to Abel whom he has murdered, and asks defiantly, "Am I my brother's keeper?" (Genesis 3–4). In churches today we see it in a different form: loyal pew-sitters excuse themselves from learning their faith properly because others seem to them better at theology than they are, and they excuse themselves from learning to live an evangelistic lifestyle (the theme of this book) because others seem to them temperamentally better suited to this than they are themselves. They think themselves humble, keeping their proper place, but in fact they are succumbing to wriggle-out-itis in face of the call of Christ. Mark, however, grasps that as a believer, a converted Christian, and a true disciple of Jesus that he is under orders to live evangelistically. He wants with all his heart to do this and to learn how best to do it, and this makes him a role model for us all.

Those who, like Mark, have not yielded to wriggle-out-itis in relation to evangelism will gain much wisdom from the pages that follow.

J. I. Packer

PREFACE

I am very thankful that you are interested in this book. But before we begin, I want to share a little information with you so you will know where I'm coming from.

I write this book, first and foremost, as a follower of Jesus. I write this book as one who is convinced that Jesus is the only way of salvation (John 14:6) and that those who come to him must place explicit faith in his person and work (Acts 4:12). I write this book as a biblicist who believes the Scriptures are inerrant and infallible. While I do not worship the Bible, I believe the God I worship has spoken and preserved what he wants the world to know about him in the Bible. Because of this conviction and the subject of this book, I write with the assumption that while you may differ from me on your view of some passages in the Bible, nevertheless, you are confident in the veracity of the Scriptures—that they are sufficient for both belief and practice.

My audience for this book is mainly other followers of Jesus. If you are not a follower of Jesus, I am very thankful that you are considering reading this book, but please keep my audience in mind as you read. Let me encourage you that the Jesus I write about is the one who went to the cross for the sins of the world and died but arose from the dead. He offers not only forgiveness for sins but hope for this life and the life to come. I would urge you, even as you are reading these words, to turn from your sinful direction away from God and turn to Jesus, believing in your heart that God raised him from the dead, and confessing him as your Lord (Romans 10:9). This book will tell you some things about Jesus, but the best place to begin reading about him is the New Testament of the Bible (start with the book of Mark). If you make the decision to follow Jesus or have questions about following him, please contact me, for I would love to hear from you.

This book is not a model-specific book on how to engage one-on-one in personal evangelism. Many excellent how-to books already exist. While practical in nature, this book attempts to establish certain parameters for evangelism by answering questions, with the understanding that within those parameters you will be sharing your faith in a way that is contextually relevant.

This book is not a book on Christian apologetics. While you will find elements of apologetics in this work, you should consult with one of the numerous excellent books available today on the topic if you are interested in apologetics.

This book is not a defense of Wesleyan/Arminian or Reformed/Calvinist theology. If you would like to read more about these theological traditions, I have included a few references at the end of this book to get you started. While I do not consider myself a five-point Calvinist, I do consider myself Calvinist in my theology related to God's sovereignty, human depravity, election, grace, and the preservation of believers until the day of their glorification. Therefore, I must add that while I find myself closer to the Reformed/Calvinist camp than the Wesleyan/Arminian camp, I have attempted to answer the questions in this book from a biblical perspective. While my biases will obviously come through from time to time, I have attempted to answer each question posed by using Scripture. Where I have found it helpful to delve into these differing theological camps, I have tried to be as fair and accurate as possible in representing both perspectives. When the Scriptures shout aloud a particular answer, I feel at liberty to herald it with great volume. But when the Scriptures speak softly or not at all to a particular question, I must also speak softly or not at all. Such issues should not trouble us, because we cannot fully grasp an infinite God with our finite minds, and if we could, faith would not be necessary (Hebrews 11:6).

I write this book as a missiologist, Baptist minister, and professor who is deeply concerned about the advancement of the gospel among the peoples of the world. Our biblical and theological foundations influence our daily practices. Orthodoxy (right belief) results in orthopraxy (right action); if not, then our orthodoxy is to be questioned.

While my name is on the cover of this book, and while I take full responsibility for the content of my writing, the publication of any such work is truly the collaborative effort of many. I want to thank my secretary, Renee Emerson, for assisting me with the indexes and numerous other administrative tasks. I must say "thank you" also to my research assistant, Matt Pierce. I greatly appreciate my friend and colleague Tim Beougher for offering his wisdom on this project as well.

This is my third book with Biblica. As always, it has been a pleasure working with the brothers and sisters with the company. I need to extend a word of appreciation to Volney James, my publisher, and to those who make up his committee, for believing in this book and my ability to write it. Thank you to John Dunham, my editor, and to his team for all their efforts as well. Thank you, Bette Smyth, for your proofing and editorial capabilities. (I appreciate you always making my grammar read real good!) My appreciation also goes out to Mike Dworak and his marketing efforts to spread the word on this book.

A great amount of thanksgiving goes to Sarah, the greatest wife and mother in the world! And I must thank Hannah, Rachel, and Joel, my three little wild children whom I love a great deal.

This book would not have been possible without the Tribe of Payne. Thank you, guys, very much.

The Lord has greatly blessed me in this project. Without him none of this would have been possible. If he had not saved me, this book would not have been written. Therefore, I must end by offering my greatest word of appreciation to the Lord.

INTRODUCTION

The conversations that run throughout this book are between two fictional characters, Roberto and Mark. Interspersed are my reflections on their interactions in light of the Scriptures. Everything has been written to assist you in being better prepared to share the good news of Jesus with others.

We learn whenever we ask questions. I believe that throughout my youth, I drove my pastors, teachers, and mentors crazy with my questions about the Scriptures. The book you hold is my attempt to respond to the most commonly asked questions about evangelism. Some of these questions have been asked across the centuries of church history; others have come about in recent years.

In this book you will meet two fictional men—Roberto, a thirty-seven-year-old insurance agent, and Mark, a twenty-two-year-old university senior and anthropology major. Roberto has been a follower of Jesus for twenty years; Mark came to faith within the last year. Shortly after Mark was baptized, Roberto started mentoring him. Every Thursday evening these men meet at a local coffee shop to discuss matters related to the Christian life. For the past few months, their weekly conversations have revolved around Mark's questions. Roberto thought this would be a good way to teach Mark the truths of the Bible, realizing that many of us learn a great deal when we are allowed to ask our most pressing questions and then are directed to Scripture for the answers.

Each chapter begins with Roberto and Mark's interaction. Their dialogue introduces the topic of the chapter, and then I address that topic from a biblical perspective. The heart of each chapter, and thus the purpose for this book, is to understand what the Bible has to say about various issues surrounding evangelism.

Now, I clearly recognize that in recent days some view doctrine as cold, stale, dry, and boring, something to be relegated to the dusty halls of ivory-tower, theological academia because it has no bearing on daily life. Such might be the case if we understand doctrine to be whim and speculation—human traditions about Jesus and his church. But biblical doctrine, that which comes from the Scriptures, is exciting and provides nourishment for the follower of Jesus (1 Timothy 4:6). The apostle Paul wrote to Titus that he should speak sound doctrine (Titus 2:1) and set an example before the other believers in his good deeds.

Without doctrine, anything goes. Doctrine is a good thing, vital to right living as kingdom citizens. Without a foundation of biblical doctrine, we are tossed back and forth by the turbulent waves and winds of human reasoning (Ephesians 4:14), not standing firm on the faith "once for all delivered to the saints" (Jude 3). Therefore, we will discover that Roberto and Mark's conversations are filled with doctrinal issues that are far from boring.

I am also aware that for some readers, the word *evangelism* conjures up fear, guilt, and the thought of narrow-mindedness. Contributing to this negative impression are the pluralism and secularism of our culture and the fact that the church has produced many poor examples of what it means to carry out the Great Commission. Despite evangelism's bad reputation, however, the church is a missional body comprised of kingdom citizens who by their very nature are missional (intentionally evangelistic in all they do). We are called to be his witnesses (Acts 1:8) and make disciples (Christ followers) of all peoples (Matthew 28:19), regardless of any ungodly impressions the world or the church have connected to evangelism. The communication of the good news of Jesus is about liberation and healing, salvation and abundant life, and restoration and peace. The world says such things are bad; God says they are good.

I have been teaching evangelism and missions courses in Bible colleges and at a seminary for over ten years. I have written numerous articles on these topics and have published a few books addressing such matters as well.

Over the past thirteen years, I have pastored churches and served on church-planting teams in Kentucky and Indiana. I simply share this information as part of my background to let you know that I believe that I have a good sense of the questions Christ's followers are asking, in the United States in particular, about matters related to evangelism. And through our eavesdropping on Roberto and Mark, we will come to understand these relevant questions and what the Bible has to say about them.

Each chapter of this book addresses a particular question and can stand alone, making this book a useful reference work as well as a book to read cover to cover. Skim the Contents pages, and if one chapter's question is relevant to your immediate situation, you might want to start reading there. The book is set up to allow you to skip around without any loss of understanding.

The end of each chapter has a few questions to help you think through the content. These also make good discussion questions if you are using the book with a small group or a class or in a mentoring relationship such as that of Roberto and Mark.

So now let us turn our attention to an unnamed city where Roberto and Mark live, work, play, and meet each week to talk about the truths of the Bible regarding evangelism.

CHAPTER 1

WHAT IS EVANGELISM, ANYWAY?

Mark rounded the corner and saw the glowing neon sign in the window at Beans. The sign seemed more distinct than usual; daylight ended earlier now that fall was here. Since early summer, he and Roberto had been meeting here on Thursday evenings at seven.

Mark, now a senior anthropology major at the university, had become a follower of Jesus only a year ago. Shortly thereafter he was baptized and became a member of The Bridge Community Church. The pastors of this newly planted church had implemented a mentoring strategy for new believers, and Mark was immediately paired up with Roberto. Such an approach to discipleship training meant a lot to Mark. He came from an agnostic home and attended church only at Christmastime, with his grandmother. He had taken courses in the New Testament as literature and the sociology of religion, but for the most part he was biblically illiterate.

Mark smiled. Now he was reading the Bible every day, meeting regularly with Roberto, and soaking up everything about his new life like a sponge.

Roberto had quickly become a close friend. He was older, thirty-seven, an insurance agent, married for twelve years and father of two. Roberto's parents immigrated to the United States when he was four years old, and he'd grown up in a strong evangelical Christian home where he was taught to fear the Lord and came to love and serve him at a young age. He was baptized at eleven but always felt he became a follower of Jesus much earlier.

Mark opened the glass door plastered with announcements for upcoming local concerts and immediately heard the sounds of Miles Davis playing over the speakers. That had to mean Dave Jazz-man Jones was working tonight. Third time this week. Business must be treating him well.

Mark spotted Roberto at a table across the crowded room. A few people had their noses buried in textbooks; others were surfing the web and catching up on e-mail. But tonight most people seemed locked into quiet conversations. Despite the crowd the shop was not too noisy.

"Hola . . . Kemo Sabe!" Such was Mark's usual attempt to poke fun at Roberto's Hispanic heritage. He always meant it in jest. Roberto knew this and at times turned the tables and joked that Mark would spend the rest of his life working at the campus pizza shop using his "valuable" anthropology degree to study people and culture.

A server brought Mark's usual cheesecake and coffee. "It's really good to see you tonight," Mark told Roberto. "How are you and the family?"

For several minutes Mark and Roberto caught up on each other's news. Then Mark said, "You know, I have been trying to be a witness for the Lord for the past several months. I've been talking to several people about Jesus. My question tonight is, What is evangelism, anyway? I thought I knew, but now I'm confused. I heard the pastor on Sunday briefly mention that we need to do evangelism and that Billy Graham did evangelism. I thought I was doing evangelism by talking to people on campus about Jesus, but I know I'm no Billy Graham!"

Roberto sipped his coffee. "Mark, evangelism is sharing the good news about Jesus, and there are lots of ways to do that. Graham spoke to crowds gathered in stadiums. Other people lead evangelistic Bible studies."

"Like Ted in the dorm." Ted was the friend who had introduced Mark to Jesus.

"Yes, and like Julie and Charles on Tuesday nights. Some people go door to door, visiting with total strangers; others do service events to connect with people in the community and witness to them. There are many ways to share the good news about Jesus."

//

Mark's question is a good place for us to begin this book about evangelism. We need a definition so that we will know what is being discussed.

To begin, let's take some time to break down Roberto's response that "evangelism is sharing the good news about Jesus." In the original Greek language in which the New Testament was written, several words can assist us in understanding the meaning of the term *evangelism*. *Euaggelizo* is used many times in the New Testament and can be translated as "I bring the good news" or "I preach." Its noun form, *euaggelion*, can be translated as "gospel" or "good news." Therefore, evangelism is preaching or delivering to others the good news about Jesus. Such communication is not limited to a pulpit or a stadium but can happen anywhere, at any time, among any people.

Jesus preached the good news of the kingdom (Matthew 4:17; Luke 4:18) and instructed his followers to do likewise (Matthew 10:7). Peter told a house full of people that Jesus "commanded us to preach" (Acts 10:42). The apostle Paul was sent to "preach the gospel" (1 Corinthians 1:17). He preached "Christ crucified" (1 Corinthians 1:23) and "Jesus Christ as Lord" (2 Corinthians 4:5). He wrote that it was unthinkable for him not to preach the gospel (1 Corinthians 9:16). Paul instructed Timothy to "preach the word" (2 Timothy 4:2), with "word" referring to God's word to humanity. The Bible notes that we are to "make disciples" (Matthew 28:19), which occurs through the preaching of the gospel (Acts 14:21).

So evangelism is simply the communication of the good news of Jesus, with the desired outcome of seeing others follow Jesus and serve him as faithful disciples together in local churches. Such is the biblical way. Although this communication involves modeling a healthy example of the Christian lifestyle and working to assimilate new followers of Jesus into churches, evangelism is *the sharing of God's message in a way others can understand so that they might turn from their sins and place their faith in Jesus.*

Such an explanation brings us to another very important matter. Evangelism is about sharing good news. Therefore we must ask, What is this good news?

And here we must return to Beans, for such is the next question at the table.

Questions to Consider

- How do you feel about the fact that we are preaching whenever we share the gospel with another person?
- Do you agree that evangelism is simply telling others the good news about Jesus with a purpose to see them begin to follow him? Why or why not?
- Why do you think the Scriptures reveal that those who come to faith in Jesus must become a part of a local church?

CHAPTER 2

WHAT IS THE GOSPEL?

"If evangelism is about sharing the good news, that assumes we have good news to share," Mark said with a smile.

"Not just any good news, but specific good news. I think what you're basically getting at is the question, What is the gospel? The word *gospel* means "good news," and it is good news."

"Yes. That's right!" He took a bite of cheesecake.

"Are you going to eat all of that?" Roberto asked.

"Every last bite. Everyone is supposed to have two to three servings of dairy every day, remember? Here I can have cheese and, factoring in the dollops of whipped cream on top, I'm knocking out two servings right here."

"Whatever!" Roberto sighed. "Where were we?"

"The good news. What is the good news—the gospel—that we share?"

//

Nelson's New Illustrated Bible Dictionary defines *gospel* as "the joyous good news of salvation in Jesus Christ."[1] As noted in chapter 1, the Greek word *euaggelion* is translated as "gospel" and "good news." The first sentence of the book of Mark reads, "The beginning of the gospel of Jesus Christ, the Son of God," with "gospel" referring to the story about Jesus.

Jesus proclaimed the gospel of the kingdom (Matthew 4:23; 9:35) and told his followers that the gospel was to be preached throughout the whole world (Matthew 24:14). Paul wrote that he was "eager to preach the gospel" (Romans 1:15), and he and Barnabas preached the good news on their church-planting journeys (Acts 14:15). The writer of Hebrews noted that "the good news came to us" (Hebrews 4:2).

The *gospel*, or "good news," is what we are to share with others. It is a message about how God's enemies become God's friends (reconciliation), prisoners bound by sin are set free (redemption), spiritually dead people are made alive (regeneration), people under God's wrath receive his mercy (propitiation), people in the kingdom of darkness move into the kingdom of light (sanctification), the guilty become acquitted (justification), and people in the family of the evil one become members of the family of God (adoption).[2] It is the message that the Creator is renewing and will renew his broken creation. It is a message about life after death and life here and now (John 10:10).

An examination of the book of Acts reveals that Jesus' life and ministry is the fulfillment of the promises God made in the Old Testament (Acts 3:18; 10:43; 26:22; 28:23). The first such promise was made in the garden of Eden—God would eventually crush the head of the serpent through the "seed" (Genesis 3:15 KJV) of the woman. This promise is continually addressed throughout the Old Testament as God worked through Abraham's descendants to bring the Savior into the world in "the fullness of time" (Galatians 4:4). It is through this Savior that people are forgiven for their sins and the created order will be restored as a new heaven and a new earth (Revelation 21:1).

Such is the good news: God loves sinners and sent Jesus to die on a cross as a sacrifice for their sins (John 3:16). Jesus' death, burial, and resurrection reveal that he alone has the power to overcome the broken relationships between the Creator and the creation. In his first letter to the Corinthians, Paul summarized the message this way:

> Now I would remind you, brothers, of the gospel I preached to you, which you received, in which you stand, and by which you are being saved, if you hold fast to the word I preached to you—unless you believed in vain. For I delivered to you as of first importance what I also received: that Christ died for our sins in accordance with the Scriptures, that he was buried, that he was raised on the third day in accordance with the Scriptures, and that he appeared to Cephas, then to the twelve. Then he

appeared to more than five hundred brothers at one time, most of whom are still alive, though some have fallen asleep. Then he appeared to James, then to all the apostles. Last of all, as to one untimely born, he appeared also to me (1 Corinthians 15:1–8).

The gospel is about God's work to bring salvation to fallen humanity. Paul noted that the gospel "is the power of God for salvation to everyone who believes" (Romans 1:16) and that Jesus became sin for us so that we could become the "righteousness of God" (2 Corinthians 5:21). In other words, Jesus, who was without sin, took our sin on himself as a sacrifice on our behalf. He took our sin and gave us his own holiness. This is good news! Though this message is considered as foolishness to some, this "foolishness of God" is able to bring about the salvation of those who believe (1 Corinthians 1:21–25).

In addition to the good news being about the forgiveness of sins, it is also a message about abundant life. Jesus declared, "I came that they may have life and have it abundantly" (John 10:10). This good news we share with others is not only about matters related to life in heaven. This good news includes the fact that we can enter into a personal relationship with the God of the universe. It is Jesus' desire that those who follow him have an abundant life here and now. This does not mean that we will have everything we want or an easy-going lifestyle. Rather, it involves having the blessings and joy of the Lord in this life and being a part of the bride of Christ forever (Revelation 21:9).

Questions to Consider

- What are the main points of the gospel?
- Jesus took our sin on himself and gave us his holiness so that we could be in the presence of a holy God (2 Corinthians 5:21). What is your response to this? How does it affect the way you communicate the gospel?

CHAPTER 3

WHAT IS REPENTANCE?

"How about we look at some of the Bible's teachings that directly relate to sharing our faith?" Roberto began.

"OK. Like what?" Mark asked.

"Well, teachings such as repentance, faith, conversion, for example."

"Sounds complicated and deep." Mark looked pensive. "I think I'm somewhat familiar with those concepts, but I'm not sure. So they are important when it comes to sharing our faith?"

"Very important, for they are essential in communicating the gospel, the good news."

"Are you telling me I must become a theologian in order to share my faith?"

Roberto heard the concern in Mark's voice. "Yes," he responded, "but not the type of theologian you have in mind. You don't need a funky black robe and little hat or to learn Latin and all that. I just want you to be a student of God's Word. I want you to think and act correctly, guided by the Scriptures. There are many voices in the world today talking about God and his Word. Some of those voices are right and good, and some of those voices are wrong and evil."

"So how do I know the difference?"

"Ahh, Grasshopper. You are asking the right question!" Roberto said with his best Asian accent. "When I was working on my degree, one of my professors told an interesting story. Before the days of high-tech gadgetry, banks were often given counterfeit bills. In an attempt to curb the influx, bank employees had to be trained how to distinguish the fake bills from the real ones."

"So what did they do?" Mark asked.

"The employees spent a great deal of time with the real bills, examining every minute feature. They became so familiar with the real deal that they could easily spot the fake if it passed through their hands."

"Cool." Mark replied. "What's the point?"

"Stay in the Word. Become an expert on the real deal. Hide God's words in your heart.[1] Be a Berean. Remember those guys? They heard Paul's teaching but did not accept it as true until they checked it out in the Scriptures.[2] In fact, you need to check the Scriptures to see if *I'm* correct or way off base, instead of simply taking my word for it."

"And if you are off base, can I call you a heretic and burn you at the stake?" Mark chuckled. "Can we start with repentance then? What is repentance? I know it involves turning from sin. I also know that I remember watching some crazy spoof on YouTube of TV preachers screaming, "Repent!" over and over again to hip-hop music."

"YouTube? Is that where you get your Bible teaching?" Roberto asked with much surprise.

Mark laughed. "No, just some comic relief!"

//

Our understanding of repentance comes from the Greek word *metanoia,* which generally means "a change of mind." Repentance is a change in direction. Imagine making a 180-degree change in course on a journey; that's a picture of repentance. Repentance involves a change in our actions, thoughts, attitudes, emotions, and will. It is not just feeling guilty for our sin but forsaking our sin.

An examination of the biblical evidence reveals numerous passages addressing repentance. God called on Israel to repent—to turn from idols and back to him because repentance brings life—and he promised that he would restore their blessings, service to him, and fellowship with him when they did. John the Baptist, Jesus, and the apostles called on people to repent, and Jesus said there is rejoicing in heaven whenever anyone does (Luke 15:7). Calling for repentance is part of the church's Great Commission (Luke 24:47), because the Lord does not wish for anyone to perish but for all to come to repentance (2 Peter 3:9).[3]

If we turn toward God as we repent, what are we turning from? Those who come to faith in Christ commit to turn from their sin nature (see the figure below). Since Adam's fall in the garden of Eden (Genesis 3:6), the entire human race has been affected by Adam's sin of disobedience (Romans 5:12). We are born with a nature to rebel against God, and out of this sin nature, we commit individual sinful behaviors, such as hatred, lust, and greed. We all sin and fall short of God's perfection (Romans 3:23). No one can make a list of all of the sins he has committed (or will commit) and repent of each one individually. While repentance does involve the turning from the evidence of the sin nature, ultimately the individual is turning from the essence of who they are as a fallen creature.

SIN
(SIN NATURE)

S I N S
(EVIDENCE OF THE SIN NATURE)

HATRED	LUST	GREED	MURDER	FALSE RELIGION
SLANDER	THEFT	FORNICATION	BROKEN RELATIONSHIPS	

FIGURE 1. EVIDENCE OF THE SIN NATURE

We sin in our actions (such as murder and theft) and in our attitudes (such as lust, hatred, jealousy). We commit sins of omission and sins of commission. Repentance is not just an intellectual agreement with God or just a rush of feelings, but a wholistic change. Wayne Grudem noted that "repentance is a heartfelt sorrow for sin, a renouncing of it, and a sincere commitment to forsake it and walk in obedience to Christ."[4]

Thomas Watson described repentance as "a grace of God's Spirit whereby a sinner is inwardly humbled and visibly reformed" and as a "spiritual medicine" that consists of six special "ingredients" summarized briefly here: First, during repentance the individual has recognition of sin. A person must know about sin before turning from it. Second, there is sorrow for sin. Knowing that God is offended leads the individual to experience sorrow for sinful actions. Individuals differ in the emotions they show when repenting, but sorrow is always present. Third, there is a confession of sin. Sin is so terrible that the human soul must purge before God. Fourth, a shame for sin is present during repentance. Fifth, a hatred for sin is felt. And finally, a turning from sin is experienced.[5]

I remember once sharing the gospel with someone who responded by asking, "Do I have to stop having sex since I'm not married?" He was not so much asking the question out of a truly repentant heart, but rather as if he could bargain with God, desiring to follow Jesus yet remain committed to his sin. In other words, he was willing to give all of himself to God except for this one area of his life. His attitude reflected that he did not truly grasp the wickedness of his sin. While there is no doubt that he would probably continue to struggle with the temptation of sexual immorality, it is one thing to struggle from a heart surrendered to the leadership of the Holy Spirit and a heart that is not. This guy reminded me of the young man that once came to Jesus, desiring salvation. When Jesus told him to surrender his finances, the man balked and turned his back on Jesus, missing out on the wealth of the kingdom (Mark 10:21). A truly repentant heart is one that has concerns about future sinful behaviors yet still surrenders the past, present, and future to Jesus.

Questions to Consider

- When you share the gospel, do you inform others about the necessity of repentance?
- How does thinking about repentance as a spiritual medicine affect your understanding of it?
- If you were witnessing to someone willing to follow Jesus but not willing to turn from a particular sin, what would you say to that person?
- If someone asked if he needed to make a list of all of the sins he had ever committed and individually repent of each, how would you respond?

CHAPTER 4

WHAT IS SAVING FAITH?

"So if repentance is turning away from our sin nature, which includes thoughts, feelings, and actions, where does belief come into the picture?" Mark asked.

"The best way to think of the relationship between belief and repentance is as two sides of the same coin." Roberto replied. "In other words, repentance is turning *from* something and belief is turning *toward* something. They happen simultaneously. And you can't have one without the other."

"So if you repent from your sin, you put your belief in Jesus at the same time?" Mark asked.

"Yes. Genuine repentance from sin includes genuine belief in Jesus. This belief is what it means to have faith in Jesus. A person does not repent today and place faith in Jesus tomorrow."

"Repentance and faith are intimately connected?" Mark asked for clarification.

"That's right," said Roberto. "Let's summarize. Again, think of the two sides of a coin. On one side there is repentance, and on the other side is faith."

Mark looked puzzled. "But aren't believers told to repent throughout their lives?"

Roberto turned to his open Bible. "That type of repentance is not for forgiveness of sins but rather for the restoration of fellowship with the Lord. In other words, when I became a believer in Jesus, that was the time when God forgave me, brought his salvation to my life, and adopted me into his family.[1] However, I will continue to sin throughout my earthly life. Whenever I do wrong, I must immediately return to my Father, confess my shortcomings to him, and turn from such sin. This is not for his forgiveness (I already have that), but that my closeness with him and his guidance in my life will not be hindered.

"Think of it this way. I was born to my parents. There is nothing that can change that biological reality. However, if I insult my parents, the closeness of our relationship will suffer. They will always remain my mom and dad, but my behavior can lead to problems in our family."

//

The writer of Hebrews noted, "And without faith it is impossible to please him, for whoever would draw near to God must believe that he exists and that he rewards those who seek him" (Hebrews 11:6). Throughout the Scriptures the Greek words used for *belief, trust,* and *faith* are similar. To have faith in Jesus is to believe in Jesus and trust him to save us.

For example, David wrote that we are to put our trust in God (Psalm 4:5; cf. 9:10; 31:14). Jesus told a woman that her faith saved her (Luke 7:50), and he told Paul that sanctification is a result of placing faith in him (Acts 26:18). Paul preached this message by declaring to everyone the need to place faith in the Lord Jesus (Acts 20:21; 24:24).

Unbelief keeps people from entering into God's salvation. Roberto told Mark that repentance and faith are two sides of the same coin because repentance involves turning from sin while faith involves turning toward Jesus for salvation. In other words, genuine repentance involves genuine faith. The object of saving faith must be in Jesus because only he can provide salvation. And the activity of saving faith involves the whole being of a person—intellect, emotions, and volition.

Saving Faith Means Faith in Jesus

The Scriptures are very clear that saving faith only comes when faith is placed in the correct object—Jesus alone. The psalmist noted that some people trust in chariots and some in horses, but he and others put their trust in the name of the Lord (Psalm 20:7). Jesus said, "I am the way, and the truth, and the life. No one comes to the Father except through me" (John 14:6). Speaking to the religious leaders and referring to Jesus, Peter and John declared, "And there is salvation in no one else, for there is no other name under heaven given among men by which we must be saved" (Acts 4:12). Paul wrote that "everyone who calls on the name of the Lord will be saved" (Romans 10:13). He reminded the Corinthian believers that they were sanctified and justified in the name of Jesus (1 Corinthians 6:11).

Saving Faith Involves Our Intellect

Our faith must have a cognitive aspect. In order to be saved we must know the facts about Jesus. For whoever wants to draw near to God must believe in him (Hebrews 11:6), and belief by definition requires an intellectual component.

Saving Faith Involves Our Emotions

In addition to an intellectual agreement with the gospel, our emotions are involved in saving faith. An emotional involvement does not mean that saving faith is always accompanied by emotional outbursts, but it does mean that we are passionate about turning from the ways of the wicked world and turning to Jesus for salvation.

Saving Faith Involves Our Volition

We must place our trust in Jesus alone for our salvation. This aspect of saving faith requires that we employ our will to diligently follow him. Our will guides our behavior, so our actions should reveal that we have substantially turned from sinful ways. This does not mean we are perfect but that we have changed the direction of our lives.

Questions to Consider
- How does knowing that repentance and faith are two sides of the same coin affect the way you will share the good news?
- How does knowing the importance of the object of our faith affect the way you will tell others about Jesus?

CHAPTER 5

WHAT IS CONVERSION?

"OK. That's helpful, Roberto," Mark said. He rocked backwards on two legs of his chair.

Roberto glanced at his watch. "I've got to run in a few minutes and get home. I have to be in the office early tomorrow, and we have family staying with us this weekend so I promised to help get the house in order. Anything else you want to chat about tonight?"

"Yeah, you said something a minute ago that caused me to think of something else. What about conversion? That's what it is called whenever someone decides to follow Jesus, right?"

"Correct," Roberto replied, finishing his coffee. "Do you understand what happens when someone experiences conversion?"

"I know that the words *to convert* are generally seen as something negative."

"You mean like coercing someone to follow a different religion?"

"Or brainwashing," Mark said.

//

In popular society the word *conversion* has developed a negative connotation. A convert is sometimes understood to be someone who was manipulated to turn from his or her religion to a new faith. And one who converts others is seen as a scoundrel, lurking around dark corners, waiting to pounce on unsuspecting passersby, blitzing them with a tirade about burning in hell and cramming a stack of gospel tracts in their hands.

But while *convert* and *conversion* have morphed into negatively viewed words among many, we need to understand that the Word of God supports both the use of these words and their meanings without the contemporary stereotypes.

While describing his own conversion experience, Paul noted that the Lord called him to open the eyes of the Gentiles "so that they may turn from darkness to light and from the power of Satan to God, that they may receive forgiveness of sins and a place among those who are sanctified by faith in me" (Acts 26:18). On their way to Jerusalem, Paul and Barnabas traveled through Phoenicia and Samaria, and described "in detail the conversion of the Gentiles, and brought great joy to all the brothers" (Acts 15:3). When closing his letter to the Romans, Paul requested that they "greet my beloved Epaenetus, who was the first convert to Christ in Asia" (Romans 16:5). In a similar fashion, Paul wrote to the Corinthians, "Now I urge you, brothers—you know that the household of Stephanas were the first converts in Achaia, and that they have devoted themselves to the service of the saints" (1 Corinthians 16:15).

Conversion is turning to Jesus. Conversion is what happens when someone repents of sin and turns toward Jesus, placing faith in him alone for salvation. Conversion is witnessed as the human element in the process of salvation whereby the individual turns under divine influence. Conversion is the result of the regenerative act of the Holy Spirit on a person's heart. We see this, for example, just prior to the planting of the church in Antioch. Luke recorded that some who left Jerusalem traveled to Antioch preaching Jesus, "And the hand of the Lord was with them, and a great number who believed turned to the Lord" (Acts 11: 21). We see other evidence of the idea of turning from the wrong way to the way of the Lord throughout the Scriptures.[1]

Conversion Is a Good Thing

Conversion is the beginning of following Jesus, revealing that we have entered into the kingdom of God. We have come out of the dominion of darkness and into the kingdom of light (Colossians 1:12–13) and received forgiveness; the old life has gone and the new life has come (2 Corinthians 5:17). Upon conversion, we have given up on the idols of this world and are now serving the true and living God (Acts 26:20; 1 Thessalonians 1:9).

Conversion Is Connected with Regeneration, Justification, and Sanctification

We must remember that while conversion is a human reaction in the salvation process, it is wed to the divine working of the Spirit. When a true conversion experience occurs, the convert has experienced *regeneration* (the new birth; see chapter 7), *justification* (being made acceptable before a holy God), and *sanctification* (being set apart for kingdom service).

We Cannot Directly Convert Anyone

While John the Baptist came to turn the Jewish people to the Lord (Luke 1:16) and James wrote that we should turn back the wanderer to the truth (James 5:19–20), such actions are indirect. In other words, we have a role to play in the conversion process, but we cannot *force* someone to convert. We can, however, serve the Lord in the conversion process if our approach is not manipulative. Coercive tactics often result in false decisions for Jesus. We must be people who gently call others to turn from their ways and to the Way.

I cannot force my children to eat; however, I can put good food before them. I can tell them that it is dinner time. I can tell them to eat. Yet they have to open their mouths, chew their food, and swallow it for themselves. So put good and appealing food before unbelievers. Tell them about it. Show them how great it is. But remember they have to eat for themselves.

Questions to Consider
- Do those outside of the church typically think of conversion in a positive or negative light? Why?
- How does knowing that you cannot force anyone to convert to Jesus affect the way you will share the gospel with others?

CHAPTER 6

DOES CONVERSION OCCUR AT ONE POINT IN TIME, OR IS IT A PROCESS?

The next week, Mark noticed the leaves on the trees were starting to show their fall colors. Sweatshirt weather had arrived.

Mark had spent much time reflecting on his last conversation with Roberto. He did not always come with a prepared question each week, but last week's encounter had raised an unanswered question. Roberto had encouraged him to e-mail any questions that came up during the week, but somehow Mark felt that tonight's question needed to be discussed face-to-face.

"Hey, man! How's it going?" Roberto began.

"I'm doing good tonight."

"Well," Roberto said.

"Huh?" Mark replied.

"*Well*."

"Well, what?"

"You are doing *well* tonight, not *good*."

Both men laughed loudly. "I hate it when you do that!" Mark said.

"I know! I know!" Roberto declared with much enthusiasm. "The Hispanic correcting White Boy's grammar! Bam!"

"I *will* make sure that I return the favor!" Mark said with a grin.

"Hey! My wife and I are making plans for a vacation this summer. We're hoping to take a cruise. Never done that before."

"Taking the kids?" Mark asked.

Roberto hesitated. "Yeah. We'll see how it goes."

"Well, I've got a question to get us started tonight," Mark said. "Been thinking about it all week."

"OK. Shoot. What do you have?"

"Last week we left off talking about conversion. So here is my question. Does conversion happen instantaneously or over a period of time?"

//

Over the years I have heard some preachers tell congregations that if they are unable to note the date of their spiritual birthday on a calendar, they are not saved. And I have heard some individuals recount the time of day, location, and detailed description of the occasion when they were converted. But thankfully our salvation is not based on our memory of the experience. For those who can remember the time and place, that is a wonderful thing. However, for other followers of Jesus, the timing of the event is known only to God.

Regeneration Happens at a Moment in Time

The Bible makes it clear that the work of the Holy Spirit on a person happens at a precise moment. This work brings about the new birth (John 3:5–8) and is understood as regeneration. Connected to regeneration is the notion of conversion, or the human response to this work of the Spirit. While different groups debate the *ordo salutis* (sequence of events in the process of salvation) repentance and faith in Christ happen within the heart at a moment in time. While a person may consider the claims of Christ over a lengthy period of time, there are no teachings in the Scriptures in which someone gradually moves out of the kingdom of darkness and over time moves into the kingdom of light. The percent of lostness in a person does not decrease over time while the percent of salvation increases—we either are in the kingdom of God or we are not. Upon death, you will not have one foot in the kingdom and the other foot in hell. Being born again is an all-or-nothing deal.

What about Jesus' Followers in the Gospels?

When did Jesus' followers experience a genuine conversion? The moment he called them to follow him? After the resurrection? While Jesus' followers were with him for almost three years, the Gospel writers inform us that the disciples did not understand the truth about Jesus' resurrection until after they saw his resurrected body (John 12:16; cf. 20:9). While scholars debate the point in time the disciples were converted based on the New Testament evidence, what is clear is that these men were followers of Jesus.

We May Not Remember the Moment of Conversion

Although I do believe that conversion happens at a moment in time, and that most people will be able to recall the experience, some may not be able to recall the precise moment. For example, when preaching to a crowd, I have extended an invitation for people to come to the front of the room to commit their life to Christ. Many have come forward and told me that they "want to be saved." I have observed them calling out to God in prayer after I explained some Bible verses (usually the same passages I used during my message). Since walking an aisle (or even praying a prayer) does not save a person, I believe that many such people were probably converted before they left their seats and walked forward. Why? Because as they sat in their seats, within their hearts, they repented and placed faith in Jesus. For example, in Acts 10:44–48, Cornelius and his household were converted while Peter was still preaching to them.

Another matter to consider is that of an individual who has been raised in a godly environment. I have encountered individuals who have told me that they do not know when they repented and placed their faith in Jesus. Rather, they say that they were always taught to fear the Lord and love him. Sometimes such people cannot remember a time when they did not love Jesus or did not want to follow him. Obviously, such individuals were not born saved, so they were converted at a young age when their hearts were sensitive to the Holy Spirit.

We Must Not Base Conversion on a Feeling

While some conversion experiences are very emotional, others are not. I have observed some people crying tears of joy upon placing their trust in Jesus, and others who showed little physical reaction. An emotional response is involved, but some people may not recall feeling the heavens shake or the earth move. Conversion is to be based on repentance toward God and faith in the Lord Jesus (Acts 20:21) and is evidenced by a life that bears the fruit of the Spirit (Galatians 5:22–23).

Questions to Consider

- Can you describe the details of your conversion and when it took place?
- Do you believe someone can be converted but not remember the day or time?
- When do you think the original eleven apostles were converted?

CHAPTER 7

WHAT DOES IT MEAN TO BE BORN AGAIN?

As Mark and Roberto discussed how conversion occurs, Mark realized he had a related question. "Is conversion the same thing as being born again?" he asked.

"They are related," Roberto responded. He set his coffee mug on the table. "Interesting that you bring up the topic of being born again. I guess it was about two weeks ago, a guy I know from another company e-mailed me about that. We've known each other for a few years, and I have had the opportunity to talk to him about Jesus a few times."

"What did he write?" Mark asked.

"He asked me if the Bible reference John 3:16 and being a born-again Christian are related. When I explained this to him, he confessed that the first time he saw a sign with John 3:16 printed on it, his first thoughts were *Who is John? What is so special about the time 3:16?* and *Is it AM or PM?*" Roberto said with a chuckle.

//

I recall driving down the interstate and seeing a sign on the side of the road: "You must be born again!" I have often wondered how many Hindus have driven by similar signs and thought, *No! I've been born again many times! And I'm tired of it!* I have watched journalists interview believers on television and identify them as born-again Christians, as if there is another kind of follower of Jesus. Many years ago, Billy Graham wrote a very popular book titled *How to Be Born Again.*

We've heard the phrase used time and time again, but do we understand what is meant by the term *born again*?

Stereotypes and pejorative concepts aside, everyone who is a follower of Jesus is born again. If someone is not born again, then he remains in his sins and separated from God. While there is support for this doctrine (regeneration) in the Old Testament, particularly related to Israel, the contemporary popularization of the term derives support from Jesus' encounter with Nicodemus in John 3. This religious leader, a Pharisee, approached Jesus at night and acknowledged that Jesus came from God. Cutting to the chase, Jesus responded, "Truly, truly, I say to you, unless one is born again he cannot see the kingdom of God" (John 3:3). What I find fascinating is that for many years Christians have asked "Are you born again?" to assess whether someone is a follower of Jesus, yet Jesus used the term only with this one man. Why? Jesus was connecting with where Nicodemus was in his spiritual journey.

Nicodemus was of Israel's religious elite, and being a descendent of Abraham was understood to be all that was necessary for a right relationship with God. Abraham and his seed were the chosen ones, God's people who had received God's law and were to be a light to the nations. And then Jesus rocked Nicodemus' world by telling him that his family tree was not sufficient to bring him into correct standing with God. Just being born to the right parents was not enough—he needed to be born again.

Peter also used the words *born again* in his first letter. He wrote, "Blessed be the God and Father of our Lord Jesus Christ! According to his great mercy, he has caused us to be born again to a living hope through the resurrection of Jesus Christ from the dead, to an inheritance that is imperishable, undefiled, and unfading, kept in heaven for you, who by God's power are being guarded through faith for a salvation ready to be revealed in the last time" (1 Peter 1:3–5). Continuing on, he noted, "Having purified your souls by your obedience to the truth for a sincere brotherly love, love one another earnestly from a pure heart, since you have been born again, not of perishable seed but of imperishable, through the living and abiding word of God" (vv. 22–23).

It is from these passages and others that we come to understand that being born again is the act of the Holy Spirit on the life of a person; it is not based on human good works but is the work of a sovereign God. We refer to this as the *doctrine of regeneration*. Paul wrote of this matter to Titus:

> For we ourselves were once foolish, disobedient, led astray, slaves to various passions and pleasures, passing our days in malice and envy, hated by others and hating one another. But when the goodness and loving kindness of God our Savior appeared, he saved us, not because of works done by us in righteousness, but according to his own mercy, by the washing of *regeneration* and renewal of the Holy Spirit, whom he poured out on us richly through Jesus Christ our Savior, so that being justified by his grace we might become heirs according to the hope of eternal life (Titus 3:3–7, emphasis added).

Regeneration is the process by which an individual becomes a new man or woman in Christ. It is a rebirth.

Writing on this doctrine, J. I. Packer noted that regeneration

- "is the 'birth' by which this work of new creation is begun, as sanctification is the 'growth' whereby it continues (1 Peter 2:2; 2 Peter 3:18)
- "changes the disposition from lawless, godless self-seeking (Romans 3:9–18; 8:7) which dominates man in Adam into one of trust and love, of repentance for past rebelliousness and unbelief, and loving compliance with God's law
- "enlightens the blinded mind to discern spiritual realities (1 Corinthians 2:14–15; 2 Corinthians 4:6; Colossians 3:10)
- "liberates and energizes the enslaved will for free obedience to God (Romans 6:14, 17–22; Philippians 2:13)."[1]

Questions to Consider

- Have you been born again? If so, are you living like it?
- Do the common stereotypes of one who has been born again trouble you? If so, why? What are some of those caricatures of a born-again Christian? Are they biblical?

CHAPTER 8

WHAT ARE WE SAVED FROM?

"OK, so sometimes we use the term *born again* when talking with others about Jesus. What about the question *Are you saved?*" Mark asked.

Roberto paused to think how he would articulate what needed to be said. "*Being saved* and *salvation* are biblical word pictures that communicate a profound theological truth."

"Like a metaphor," Mark clarified.

"Yeah. I think you could say that. But more than simply a metaphor, Mark. The word *saved* helps us better understand a divine concept. God chose to use this concept to communicate his truth to us."

Mark leaned in. "When we talk about someone being saved, we mean they are saved from something. Are we talking about being saved from sin and going to heaven?"

Roberto nodded. "Yes, but more than simply being saved from sin and going to heaven."

"Saved from hell?"

"Yes. But more than that too," Roberto replied. "Let's look at some biblical passages before we leave tonight."

//

I remember once hearing a friend of mine tell his story of attempting to communicate the gospel to his father. Shortly after my friend's own conversion experience, he returned home and asked his father, "Are you saved?" My friend was a part of a faith tradition where such a question was commonplace. He assumed that his unbelieving father would clearly understand the question. However, his father responded by asking, "Saved from what?"

It is important that we understand what the Bible says we are saved from.

Saved from the Penalty of Sin

While God is an infinitely loving God, he is also an infinitely just God. And in his divine economy, sin exacts a penalty—his eternal wrath. A broken law demands justice. When Jesus died on the cross, he suffered our punishment for sin; he suffered the eternal wrath of God. By placing our faith in Jesus, we are saved from the judgment to come when sinners will be judged for their sins and cast into hell (Revelation 20:11–15). While we will have to give an account of what we have done with the great salvation Jesus provided us (Romans 14:12), our sins will not be held against us (Colossians 1:14).

Saved from the Power of Sin

When we place our faith in Jesus, we are saved from sin's power over us. The Holy Spirit begins to work in our lives to make us like Christ. This is a lifelong process of becoming righteous like Christ that involves getting rid of old sinful habits such as lying, stealing, and gossiping, and acquiring the Christlike qualities of honesty, mercy, and love. As we live in the power of the Holy Spirit, the power of sin no longer controls us (Galatians 5:16–26).

Saved from the Presence of Sin

When we place our faith in Jesus, we believe that one day we will be completely free from the presence of sin. That perfect state of holiness will be fully realized when we are finally in the presence of God. Revelation 21 gives us a glimpse of this great hope of our salvation: "And I heard a loud voice from the throne saying, 'Behold, the dwelling place of God is with man. He will dwell with them, and they will be his people, and God himself will be with them as their God. He will wipe away every tear from their eyes, and death shall be no more, neither shall there be mourning, nor crying, nor pain anymore, for the former things have passed away.' And he who was seated on the throne said, 'Behold, I am making all things new.' Also he said, 'Write this down, for these words are trustworthy and true.'" (vv. 3–5).

Saved from Satan

Closely connected to salvation is protection from God's ultimate enemy, Satan. While Satan will attack the children of God, we are secure in the Father's hand. Jesus commented on this aspect of our salvation when he stated, "My sheep hear my voice, and I know them, and they follow me. I give them eternal life, and they will never perish, and no one will snatch them out of my hand. My Father, who has given them to me, is greater than all, and no one is able to snatch them out of the Father's hand" (John 10:27–29). As followers of Jesus, we have been delivered from the kingdom of darkness into the kingdom of Christ, from the power of Satan to the power of God. Revelation 20:10 tells us that a day is coming when Satan will be cast into hell forever. We know that until then Satan will come against us; but we will never lose the salvation and protection that Jesus alone provides.

Saved from Self

Another aspect of salvation is being saved from our own destructive self. We are saved from a life lived according to our own desires and rebellious ways. Jesus said that he came so that we "may have life and have it abundantly" (John 10:10). While salvation is clearly related to our future eternal reality, we *absolutely must not forget that our salvation begins here and now.* This salvation provides us with guidance and wisdom regarding our life on earth. The Good Shepherd who promised this abundant life is also with us and concerned with every aspect of our lives. He cares about who we marry, where we go to school, where we work, what house we purchase, how we raise our children, what we do with our money, how we think about life, where we go on vacation, what we do for fun, how we deal with the unruly neighbors next door, and *every other single aspect of our lives.*

While some have argued against Pascal's famous wager, I have to say that I like it. What was his wager? In my abbreviated understanding, this French philosopher was challenged by unbelievers who said that God does not exist, and thus Jesus is a farce and salvation a foolish concept. Pascal's response was something like this: I'm going to place my bet on the existence of God. If I win the bet and this God is who he claimed to be, then look at what I have gained! If I lose the bet and all of this theistic stuff is just a myth, then look at what I have gained from following after him in this life!

Extrapolating from Pascal, even if God does not exist and salvation is not true and heaven is only found in fairy tales, the way of Jesus offers something beneficial to living life in this difficult world. We can have peace of mind and sleep at night. We do not have to worry about where our food and clothing will come from. We have an ethic that guides life to keep us from the social, physical, and psychological problems that generally arise from jealousy, envy, foolishness, wastefulness, drunkenness, sexual immorality, lust, selfishness, anger, lying, theft, and so on. But the good news is that this message of God's love is true.

One criticism that has been brought against followers of Jesus is that we are so heavenly minded that we are no earthly good. Unfortunately, for many years, much of the church has communicated that salvation is simply a fire-insurance policy to be redeemed at some future date after this life is over. With a message such as this, it is no wonder so many believers, after coming to faith in Jesus, fail to live according to the good works that God prepared beforehand "that we should walk in them" (Ephesians 2:10). False teaching about this great salvation is a detriment to the expansion of the kingdom.

Questions to Consider
- How does knowing what we are saved from influence the way you will communicate the good news to others?
- How does knowing that salvation begins here and now affect the way you will communicate the good news to others?

CHAPTER 9

IF GOD IS IN CONTROL, WHY DO WE NEED TO SHARE THE GOSPEL?

Mark and Roberto continued to meet each week, always having lively discussions related to life and following Jesus. The days of fall continued on. For Mark, it would not be long before final-exams week was upon him. Roberto and his family took a weekend get-away to the mountains to see the fall colors.

Mark was always surprised at how slowly Thursday evenings seemed to come around—he truly enjoyed his mentoring meetings and anticipated each one. Roberto's knowledge of the Scriptures impressed him, but what made an even greater impression was Roberto's lifestyle; he practiced what he preached. No, he wasn't perfect, and both Roberto and Mark knew this to be true. Mark remembered several occasions when Roberto confessed shortcomings to him and also asked for prayer. Every time Roberto revealed such transparency, Mark was both impressed and surprised—impressed that his mentor was willing to admit his struggles, surprised at how Roberto did not fear that his honesty would turn Mark away.

In fact, Roberto's candidness had a magnetic effect. The first time Mark heard Roberto talk about his struggles, Mark said, "What you did just now— most people don't act that way. You know, the superior showing weakness to the inferior. In fact, the author of a business leadership textbook I read last semester noted that such action is no way to maintain a positional authority over someone."

Roberto did not disagree with the author's perspective but only declared, "The principles of this world don't always apply to the kingdom of God. I serve a king who washed the feet of his disciples." Such words were forever etched in Mark's mind.

Slowing his car in front of the shop, Mark was able to locate a good parking spot, a rare find on a Thursday night. Roberto was already inside with coffee in hand.

This week Roberto started the conversation. "I've got one for you," he said with confidence in his voice.

"OK. Shoot!" Mark replied, lifting a forkful of caramel apple pie.

"This past Sunday the message was on God being in control of everything in the universe."

"Sovereignty!" Mark blurted.

"Yes. OK, now that we know that the Bible teaches that God is sovereign and that nothing happens apart from his will, what about evangelism?"

"What about evangelism?" Mark repeated.

"If God is in control of everything, then why do we need to share the gospel?" Roberto ended his question with a slight grin that Mark had seen several times before. Roberto knew the answer but was challenging Mark to think about it.

"I hate it when you start going Socrates on me," Mark said, laughing. "Well, I guess if God is sovereign over everything that would include getting the gospel to people. . . . So I guess God is sovereign over his work of salvation in the world as well? I know he has commanded us to share the good news. . . . So I guess that's why we tell others about Jesus."

"Is that your final answer?" Roberto asked, attempting to imitate Regis Philbin.

"Sure. Yes."

"I'll give you an *A* for effort this time. But there's a little more to it as well. Let's take a look at some Scripture passages." Roberto opened his Bible and flipped through a few pages.

//

Roberto's question to Mark is a good one: If God is sovereign, why do we need to share the gospel? Shouldn't God be able to save those he wishes, regardless of what I do or don't do?

The first thing we need to keep in mind is that the communication of the gospel message is critical to the mission of God in the world. The apostle Paul noted that "the word of the cross is folly to those who are perishing, but to us who are being saved it is the power of God" (1 Corinthians 1:18). Paul understood that the gospel message, or "word of the cross," is the means by which people come to believe in Jesus. It is a manifestation of God's power in the world. Paul noted that he was not ashamed of this good news, "for it is the power of God for salvation to everyone who believes" (Romans 1:16). This gospel message is the only message that brings people into the kingdom of God, providing abundant and eternal life.

Ordaining the Means

It is true that the Lord is sovereign and that nothing happens in the universe apart from his perfect will (Ephesians 1:11). Mark, talking with Roberto, also was correct when he noted that we share the gospel with others because God has commanded his church to do that. Numerous times throughout the Scriptures we read that the Lord commands to us to be his witnesses, telling others about the good news. We are to "make disciples" (Matthew 28:19). Luke recorded that we are to preach the gospel in all the world (Luke 24:46–49). John noted that Jesus sends us out to share the gospel (John 20:21). In Acts, Luke wrote that we are to be Jesus' witnesses throughout the world (Acts 1:8), with such witnessing involving talking about what we've personally seen, heard, and experienced.

In addition to specific commands, we also see a multitude of examples of Jesus in the Gospels and the apostolic church in Acts telling others about the gospel.

Therefore, while God is sovereign over his creation, he has commanded his followers to share the gospel with others. He has ordained the means to accomplish his plan in the world. And what is that means? In his perfect plan, he has determined that his church will preach the gospel to the world.

The apostle Paul, writing to the Roman Christians, commented on the relationship of this chosen means of sharing and responding to the gospel: "For 'everyone who calls on the name of the Lord will be saved.' How then will they call on him in whom they have not believed? And how are they to believe in him of whom they have never heard? And how are they to hear without someone preaching?" (Romans 10:13–14).

Paul's point here is that everyone who calls out to the Lord in repentance and faith will be forgiven of his sins and be saved. However, he also analyzed one of his own statements to ask his readers if it is possible for people to call out to God for salvation if they do not know about him and his salvation. Obviously, Paul anticipated that his readers would respond with a clear no. He then asked two more questions to show that in order for unbelievers to hear and believe in Jesus, someone must go and tell them about him.

What we see here is that God has ordained the means by which his good news is to spread: through the mouths of his people. If no one shares the gospel, no one will come to faith in Jesus.

But you could be thinking, *Paul wrote that* someone *must preach to them, and I'm no preacher. I don't pastor a church.* But hold on a minute. Preaching is simply sharing the gospel with others; it is evangelism in action—whether it happens from a pulpit or at a table in a restaurant. Preaching is required of all kingdom citizens and is not just for professionals.

A Better Means?

It is easy for some of us to think that surely there is a more efficient and better way to spread the gospel. After all, we're only human and make mistakes. Right? I mean, come on, if the gospel is the greatest story ever told, then we're definitely not worthy to communicate such truth. Correct?

It is correct that we make mistakes and that on our own we're not worthy to carry such a great message. However, it is incorrect to believe that there is a better way. The Lord uses his children—warts and all—in sharing his love with others. But because of Christ, though we are jars of clay, we contain a great treasure (2 Corinthians 4:7). Remember, it is a tremendous honor and blessing to be able to be involved in working with the God of the universe in carrying out his plan of salvation in the world.

The Bible reminds us that God's ways are not our ways and his thoughts are not our thoughts (Isaiah 55:8). The Lord is glorified when his people share his love with his creation. In God's economy, he has chosen the foolish things of the world to shame the wise and the weak things to shame the strong (1 Corinthians 1:27). When we obey God by telling others the good news about

Christ, God uses us to bring others into his kingdom. God's plan done his way in his time and strength is his best for us and for his glory.

Questions to Consider

- Have you ever struggled with God's chosen plan for communicating the gospel to others? If so, what were the difficulties?
- Are you now willing to faithfully follow God's plan for sharing his love with others by being that means of communication? If not, why not?

CHAPTER 10

WHAT IS ELECTION?

Mark arched his back and stretching his arms overhead. With a sigh of clarity, he summarized, "OK, so I understand that we share the gospel with others because that is the message that brings people into the kingdom and that God is the most glorified when his people, as messed up as we are, share his love with others."

Roberto did not respond, sensing that Mark had another question in mind. He welcomed the unscripted time of their meeting each week, knowing the only constant element was an opening question and a time of prayer before they quit. He always thought of their time together like driving down a freeway with a number of possible exit ramps—he never knew which exit they would pick or what turns and roads it would lead to.

"This issue of God's sovereignty raises another question in my mind," Mark said.

Roberto smiled. "I think I know where you are going next."

"If God is sovereign, does that mean he has chosen some to go to heaven and some to go to hell? What about free will? Do people have free will, or are we just a bunch of robots? When we share the gospel with others, we challenge them to turn from their sin nature and turn to Jesus, but if they can't, then it seems as if we're wasting our time."

"Great questions!" Roberto exclaimed. "A bunch of great questions."

Mark leaned forward once again. He was very interested in reading what Roberto would show him in the Bible.

"Well, Mark, I wish we had time to discuss your questions, but it looks as if we're out of time and will have to take them on next week," Roberto said with a laugh. He always knew how to tease Mark.

"Shut up!" Mark exclaimed with a smile. "We've got at least forty-five minutes!" "OK. Let's take a look at the Scriptures." Roberto took a deep breath. "But somehow I don't think forty-five minutes will be enough time."

//

There are many passages in the Scriptures that either explicitly or implicitly teach the doctrine of *election*. While some are quick to ignore the matter of election or bemoan it, we should take great comfort and encouragement in it. Yes, this doctrine is a part of the mystery of God. But the truth of the matter as related to evangelism is that it is the only guarantee that people will come to faith in Jesus.

Election is the doctrine that God in his sovereignty has chosen both individuals and groups (for example, Israel and the church) for a specific purpose for his glory. Particularly related to evangelism, election is God's choice of those who will be saved. Closely related to election is the doctrine of *predestination*, which can be defined as God determining in eternity past to save (elect) some while allowing others to go their own way.

The Scriptures are very clear that God's choices are not based on human merit. He chooses out of his own independent counsel and undeserved favor. While I recognize that election and predestination are a smack in the face to the political correctness of a highly individualistic, equal-opportunity, American culture (but so is the call to put explicit faith in Jesus *alone* for salvation), these doctrines are found in the Bible. We all deserve God's just and eternal wrath for our sins, but some of us receive his mercy, yet not because of any good work in us but simply out of his will.

For example, in his letter to the Ephesian Christians, Paul wrote, "Blessed be the God and Father of our Lord Jesus Christ, who has blessed us in Christ with every spiritual blessing in the heavenly places, even as he chose us in him before the foundation of the world, that we should be holy and blameless before him. In love he predestined us for adoption as sons through Jesus Christ, according to the purpose of his will, to the praise of his glorious grace, with which he has blessed us in the Beloved" (Ephesians 1:3–6).

It is important to note that Paul wrote in this passage that God chose the believers in him to be holy and blameless even before the world was created.

And it was out of his love that he predestined the believers to be adopted by him as his children through Christ. All of this was according to his purpose and will. It is clear that God chose believers (predestined them to be adopted as his children) long before they were born—before they were ever able to do anything good or bad.

Another passage to help us understand this great truth of election, particularly related to predestination, is found in Paul's letter to the Roman Christians: "For those whom he foreknew he also predestined to be conformed to the image of his Son, in order that he might be the firstborn among many brothers. And those whom he predestined he also called, and those whom he called he also justified, and those whom he justified he also glorified" (Romans 8:29–30).

I like what Lewis A. Drummond noted about this matter of predestination: "Whatever the Bible means by predestination, it is God's way of saving the most people possible. We must never forget: the Father's will is that none 'perish, but that all should come to repentance' (2 Peter 3:9, KJV). That basic truth must be kept in the forefront."[1]

Election and Predestination in the Bible

So that you may see the significance of these doctrines, I have listed several passages related to election and predestination.

Passages on Election

- "All that the Father gives me will come to me, and whoever comes to me I will never cast out. For I have come down from heaven, not to do my own will but the will of him who sent me. And this is the will of him who sent me, that I should lose nothing of all that he has given me, but raise it up on the last day. . . . No one can come to me unless the Father who sent me draws him. And I will raise him up on the last day" (John 6:37–39, 44).
- "Since you have given him authority over all flesh, to give eternal life to all whom you have given him" (John 17:2).
- "Though they were not yet born and had done nothing either good or bad—in order that God's purpose of election might continue,

not because of works but because of him who calls—she was told, 'The older will serve the younger.' As it is written, 'Jacob I loved, but Esau I hated.' What shall we say then? Is there injustice on God's part? By no means! For he says to Moses, 'I will have mercy on whom I have mercy, and I will have compassion on whom I have compassion.' So then it depends not on human will or exertion, but on God, who has mercy" (Romans 9:11–16).

- "Who saved us and called us to a holy calling, not because of our works but because of his own purpose and grace, which he gave us in Christ Jesus before the ages began" (2 Timothy 1:9).
- "And all who dwell on earth will worship it, everyone whose name has not been written before the foundation of the world in the book of life of the Lamb who was slain." (Revelation 13:8)[2]

Passages on Predestination

- "And when the Gentiles heard this, they began rejoicing and glorifying the word of the Lord, and as many as were appointed to eternal life believed" (Acts 13:48).
- "For those whom he foreknew he also predestined to be conformed to the image of his Son, in order that he might be the firstborn among many brothers. And those whom he predestined he also called, and those whom he called he also justified, and those whom he justified he also glorified" (Romans 8:29–30).
- "He chose us in him before the foundation of the world, that we should be holy and blameless before him. In love he predestined us for adoption as sons through Jesus Christ, according to the purpose of his will" (Ephesians 1:4–5).
- "In him we have obtained an inheritance, having been predestined according to the purpose of him who works all things according to the counsel of his will" (Ephesians 1:11).

Across the centuries many wise followers of Jesus have wrestled with the truths of God's election and individual freedom (see chapter 12). While there are differing understandings of election, all evangelicals agree that God takes the initiative in beginning the salvation process. The two most common traditions among evangelicals are those of the Wesleyan/Arminian and the

Reformed/Calvinist perspectives. The Wesleyan/Arminian perspective argues that God takes the initiative for everyone in the world, and the believer chooses God. According to the Reformed/Calvinist perspective, God takes the initiative for the elect, with God choosing the believer. For Wesleyans/Arminians, God in eternity past looked down the corridors of time for those who would receive his salvation and elected them to be saved, based on how they would respond to the gospel. The Reformed/Calvinist tradition, however, argues that God in eternity past elected specific people to be saved, not based on how they would respond but purely out of his divine prerogative, known only to himself.

According to both perspectives, the total number of the elect in heaven is known only to God. Whether the Wesleyan/Arminian or the Reformed/Calvinist tradition is correct, at the end of time, the total number of believers in heaven will be the number of the elect.[3] And according to both traditions, the Lord has not chosen to reveal that number to the church. Rather, he has simply commanded the church to preach to every creature, so that as many as have been appointed to eternal life may believe (Acts 13:48).

While both traditions make excellent points on this doctrine and have excellent biblical support for many of their tenants, I believe the pendulum of the biblical evidence is pointing more in the direction of the Reformed/Calvinist tradition. An examination of the verses listed earlier in this section, the biblical evidence for the sovereignty of God, and the extent of our sin nature leads me to this conclusion. While at one time in my spiritual journey I made strong arguments for the Wesleyan/Arminian tradition (and was adamantly opposed to the Reformed/Calvinist tradition), as I began to study the Scriptures and weigh the arguments from both camps, I became more convinced of the Reformed/Calvinist tradition on the matter of God's election and work in salvation.

Some Matters to Keep in Mind

Some struggle with the notion of God's sovereignty and the individual's freedom of choice to follow Jesus. Because these two concepts can seem contradictory, over the centuries the church has attempted to reconcile them. The reality is that they cannot be (and do not need to be) reconciled, as if they were at odds with one another. While I find limitations in both the Wesleyan/Arminian and the Reformed/Calvinist traditions, there are no limitations with the Scriptures. God is not divided, just mystery.

God Is Mystery

If God is mystery, then we must be willing to live with what is mysterious. I can't explain how God created the universe, healed the blind, fed the five thousand, died a substitutionary death on the cross, and arose from the dead; but I accept those facts by faith and live by faith. The Bible declares that God is sovereign over everything, and this includes his creation and salvation. The Bible also declares that we must repent and place faith in Jesus for salvation; all must repent and believe. So on the one hand, God chooses some who will be saved, and on the other hand, he calls everyone to repent and be saved. And those who do not repent will spend eternity in hell because of their sinfulness and lack of repentance. And God remains completely just and good in doing so.

Therefore, where the Scriptures are not as clear on certain matters, I must admit the finitude of my understanding, trust in the Lord, and simultaneously hold to the doctrines of election and predestination while calling people to repent and place their faith in Jesus. Just as an airplane has two wings to keep it aloft, the Scriptures hold election and human choice together, with both being necessary for salvation. Remember, there are secret things belonging only to God (Deuteronomy 29:29). And it is to God's glory to conceal certain things from us (Proverbs 25:2). Paul writing on this difficult topic summed up the matter when he noted, "Oh, the depth of the riches and wisdom and knowledge of God! How unsearchable are his judgments and how inscrutable his ways!" (Romans 11:33).

Jesus Saves All Who Come

Jesus was very clear that "no one knows the Father except the Son and anyone to whom the Son chooses to reveal him" (Matthew 11:27). Following this statement, Jesus invited all to come to him: "Come to me, all who labor and I will give you rest" (v. 28). He will in no way turn anyone away who comes to him in repentance and faith.

I fear that someone reading this chapter will assume that God's election of some is similar to choosing teams on the playground. Some kids want to be chosen to be on one team and not the other. When the captain of the undesirable team selects one of the kids there is a sense of "Aw, man! No way! I did not want to be on this team!" Here is the practical reality of election: No one will ever enter heaven against his will, kicking and screaming, "I don't want to go!" And no one will ever enter hell kicking and screaming, "God, why did you not pick me to be on your team? I wanted to be on your team, but you rejected me! Why could I not have been one of the elect?"

The Doctrine of Election Is Encouraging and Motivating

Knowing that God will save the elect should encourage and motivate us in our evangelism. God's plan will not fail to bring people into his kingdom, and we can be part of that successful process! Some New Testament scholars conclude that God's words to Paul in Corinth were to encourage and motivate him for the sake of the elect (Acts 18:9–10). Paul also wrote to Timothy that in spite of his hardships, including persecution, "I endure everything for the sake of the elect, that they also may obtain the salvation that is in Christ Jesus with eternal glory" (2 Timothy 2:10).

The Doctrine of Election Is Liberating

Knowing that God alone is the author of salvation and in control of it, we can rest, knowing that the salvation of souls is not dependent on us. We cannot save anyone. While we may use the term *soul winner* to describe someone who is evangelistic, the Scriptures present the Holy Spirit as the only soul winner, not you or me. We are only responsible for preaching the gospel, praying, and pleading with people (Romans 10:1, 14–17; 2 Corinthians 5:18–20). If we have been faithful to bear witness to the gospel, then we can rest that God will be faithful to do his part. While there is a place for apologetics and being prepared to give a reason for the hope that we have (1 Peter 3:15), we can rest knowing the salvation of a person is not dependent on whether we can argue them into the kingdom. Effective witnessing is being faithful to share the gospel and leaving the results to God.

The Doctrine of Election Is No Excuse for Not Sharing the Gospel

We have been commanded to proclaim the good news—case closed. Some believers might assume that since all the elect come to salvation sooner or later, it doesn't really matter how much or how little we witness. That attitude is wrong on numerous levels. First, it removes the urgency of getting the gospel to people. Second, we are not commanded to go around trying to figure out who is and who is not the elect. We are called to share the gospel with anyone, anywhere, and anytime. Third, we do not know when the elect will come to faith.

God Desires the Salvation of All People

While some will not be saved because of their rebellion against a holy and loving God, the Lord does desire the salvation of the world and takes no delight in the suffering of the wicked (Ezekiel 18:23, 32; 33:11). The righteous judge must carry out his verdict on the unrepentant but is saddened by the penalty that falls upon his beloved creation. Paul wrote that God "desires all people to be saved and to come to the knowledge of the truth" (1 Timothy 2:4). And Peter reminds us that the Lord is patient and delaying the day of judgment, "not wishing that any should perish, but that all should reach repentance" (2 Peter 3:9). God's desire should become our desire.

Questions to Consider

- Do you believe that God's election of individuals to salvation is the means by which the most people will be saved? Why or why not?
- Are you troubled by the doctrine of election? If so, why?
- Does knowing the doctrine of election offer you encouragement in your personal evangelistic encounters? If so, how? If not, why not?
- Do you tend to be more Wesleyan/Arminian or more Reformed/Calvinist in your understanding of election? Why? What biblical passages can you provide to support your perspective?

CHAPTER 11

DOES A LOVING GOD SEND PEOPLE TO HELL?

"Of course, this leads to an obvious question," Mark said.

"Yes, I know. Go ahead and ask," Roberto replied.

"Does the matter of predestination and election mean that the all-loving God sends people to hell?" Mark asked. "You know, I've encountered this question recently. Last weekend I had lunch at my uncle Ted's house. He and I were eating in the living room while watching the game—"

"Ugh! Terrible game," Roberto said.

"Uncle Ted asked me if my church did anything special for Halloween this year. I told him about our community outreach event and getting prepared for our Thanksgiving food distribution."

"OK . . ."

"He said that he thought it was good for a church to help the community and especially the needy. Then out of the blue, he said, 'I could not serve a God who sends people to hell.'"

"And how did you respond?" Roberto asked.

"I was like, 'Wow! Where did that come from?' I asked him what he meant. He said, 'Well, if God is all-loving, then why does he send people to hell to burn for eternity?' I tried to answer his question honestly, but I felt my response wasn't what it should have been. Since we're on the topic, it would be good to talk about this."

//

Mark's uncle asked a question that many have asked before: How can an all-loving God send someone to hell? Is this a contradiction? Does God take delight in the sufferings of others? Is God a liar—is he not all-loving as he says? Let's take a moment to look at some Scripture passages related to this question.

Hell Is a Real Place

While some scholars have attempted to argue against the reality of hell, the Bible is clear that hell is a real place. Jesus and the apostles had much to say about hell. The Scriptures teach that hell is

- a place of torment (Luke 16:23).
- a place of eternal agony (Revelation 20:10).
- a place of unquenchable fire (Mark 9:43).
- eternal and should be avoided (Matthew 18:8).
- created for Satan and his demons (Matthew 25:41).
- a place where some people will be sent (Matthew 25:41).
- a place of eternal destruction for those who do not know God and obey him (2 Thessalonians 1:8-9).
- for those who do not have their names written in the Book of Life (Revelation 20:15).
- contrasted with the wonderful eternal life with the Lord (Matthew 25:46).

We Are All Hell-Bent Sinners

What does the Bible teach about human nature apart from God's grace? Simply put, you and I and everyone since Adam and Eve are born walking the path to hell and do not have Jesus on our radar screens. None of us knows how to buy a stairway to heaven. Paul wrote, "None is righteous, no, not one; no one understands; no one seeks for God. All have turned aside; together they have become worthless; no one does good, not even one. . . . All have sinned and fall short of the glory of God" (Romans 3:10–12, 23). What does this mean? Because of our sin nature, we have failed to live up to the divine standard of perfection. It means that we're all separated from God; there is nothing good in us to earn God's forgiveness; we are rebels against a holy God and going to hell—and this loving and holy God is correct in bringing his judgment against us.

God Is Loving and Holy

God is infinitely loving, for he is love (1 John 4:16). He loved the world so much that he gave his one and only son as a sacrifice for the sins of the world (John 3:16). While there are numerous other passages throughout the Bible that address the love of God, the fact that he is all-loving must be viewed in light of the fact that he is all-holy (Leviticus 19:2; Isaiah 6:3; Revelation 4:8). He is perfect, without sin, total purity. He is so holy that Moses was not able to look at God's face of glory without being consumed by it—like getting too close to the sun (Exodus 33:17–23).[1]

God Is a Just Judge

God is also infinitely just. He does not play favorites in his judgments (Psalm 9:4). And a single sin against an infinitely holy and just God demands eternal payment. He does not weigh our deeds in a balance to see if our good deeds outweigh our bad deeds and make us eligible for heaven. Even the very best we can do is like filthy rags in God's sight (Isaiah 64:6 KJV). And with sin comes judgment. And the verdict is that we are all guilty (Romans 3:23).

This loving yet holy God and impartial judge must bring judgment and sentence to those who have trespassed against his standard. He has drawn a line in the sand, so to speak, and we have stepped over it by disobeying his commands. God is not a judge who can be bribed. He does not look the other way because we were having a bad day when we broke his universal laws. We can plead insanity. We can argue, "I'm only human; I'm not God!" We can rightly state, "I'm not perfect!" But the verdict is that we are guilty and the payment is eternal death. For an infinitely loving and holy God to overlook one single sin in the history of humanity would contradict his love, holiness, and justice, and he would then cease to be God.

God Is Gracious

God is also infinitely gracious. He knew that there was no hope for us apart from his intervention. While he could not contradict himself and his perfect standard, only he could take the eternal punishment for our infinite offense. Someone had to pay for our crimes—and Jesus was that someone. He took our punishment so that we could have peace with him (Isaiah 53:5). He saved us from his own wrath.

Jesus took our wickedness so that we could become righteous before God (2 Corinthians 5:21). "For God did not send the Son into the world to condemn the world, but in order that the world might be saved through him" (John 3:17). The person who places faith in Jesus for forgiveness is not condemned to hell. However, the person who does not place faith in him is judged already because God's wrath stays on him and is not removed (John 3:35–36).

So from the Scriptures we see that the all-loving God does not send anyone to hell because he is a diabolical, megalomaniacal dictator. People walk themselves to hell by staying on the road to hell until they die, refusing to take advantage of God's only provision for escape—Jesus. People go to hell because they refuse to trust in Jesus as the payment for their eternal offenses against an all-holy, all-loving, all-just, all-gracious God. We love the darkness more than the light because our deeds are evil (John 3:19–20).

Why would anyone willingly drive on the highway to hell? Because we want to be god over our own world. It is the ultimate idolatry—loving our evil over God's goodness. Rather than casting ourself on the God who loves us, we refuse his gift of forgiveness, follow our own desires, and receive the just punishment for sinning against the holy Creator of the universe.

Earlier in this chapter, I stated that God does not delight when the wicked suffer but desires that all people come to repentance and find forgiveness for their sins. Yet many refuse to do things his way and come to him for life (John 5:40), and as a result spend eternity separated from him in hell.

Questions to Consider

- How does knowing that God is all-loving, all-holy, and all-just affect your understanding of how he views sin and human beings?
- If someone asked you, "How can a loving God send someone to hell?" how would you respond in your own words?

CHAPTER 12

WHAT IS THE ROLE OF FREE WILL IN SALVATION?

Mark refilled his coffee cup and sat down again. "OK, I'm with you that people spend eternity separated from God because of their unwillingness to repent and place faith in Jesus. But let's come back to the question of election. How is election fair?"

"What's not fair about it?" Roberto asked, but he knew what Mark was thinking.

"How is it fair that only some people are the elect and others are not? If you are not elect, then you are sent to hell, right?"

"Mark, that's an excellent question—one that has been asked for centuries. Here's what we know just from our discussion tonight: God is loving, holy, and just. God loves his creation, but we are sinners. A sin against this eternal God is an eternal offense with eternal consequences. Jesus is the sacrifice for our sins, paying the penalty for our eternal trespass and providing us with eternal forgiveness.

"As we discussed a moment ago, election and human freedom are mysteries, locked in the heart of God. But let's think for a moment before we look at some passages. Americans typically believe that all people are created equal and have the *right* to equality and the pursuit of happiness. Then we apply this same line of thinking to God and salvation. But we do *not* have an inalienable right to salvation, to be God's friend. The hard truth is that we all deserve hell, but God in his sovereign mercy has decided to save some. Therefore, if God desires to elect some (according to his divine choice) while allowing others to go their own way, we are quick to tell God that this is not fair. Are you following me?"

Mark nodded.

"But what is fair? It would be fair if God sent everyone to hell. No one is good enough to earn God's forgiveness or favor. Right?"

Mark nodded again.

"So if God decides to extend mercy to some[1] and simply follows through with his perfect justice on others, how is that an issue of fairness, when fairness would be for this offended God to allow all people to go their own way apart from him, with no one receiving forgiveness?"

"I hear you. But it still does not seem fair to me," Mark confessed.

"I know what you mean. But was it fair for innocent Jesus to be punished for the sins of the world? Yet he willingly offered to take our place of punishment so we could be declared not guilty in God's court. He took our sin and gave us his own righteousness. Is that fair?" Roberto got tears in his eyes. "We must remember that while we don't completely understand the ways of God, his plan is the best plan to bring the most people into heaven and bring glory to his name."

Mark said nothing.

"I don't understand everything," Roberto continued. "But I do understand that while the Bible contains numerous passages related to election and predestination, it also contains numerous passages calling all people to repent and place their faith in Jesus. Let's take a look at those as we think about free will and salvation."

//

I think Mark and Roberto just struck a chord that initially has a very dissonant ring with most people. Yet as we begin to look at the Scriptures, I think the reverberation of that chord will begin to sound more beautiful to the ears of followers of Jesus. Again, while we will not be able to explain such a mystery (as with other divine mysteries), I do believe our faith will be strengthened and our understanding of evangelism improved. So let's begin.

What is the relationship of free will to the salvation process? In other words, when I share the gospel with others, are they able to use any free will to respond, in light of the fact that the Bible teaches that God elects specific people to salvation?

Please understand that the debates surrounding the relationship of election and free will have been ongoing for centuries. (And since my publisher has foreordained that there is a page limit to this book, I cannot exert my free will to write as extensively on this topic as I would desire!)

The Scriptures have no problem holding in tandem the fact that all people are commanded to repent and place faith in Jesus for salvation *and* the fact that God is sovereign in electing people to salvation. One legendary pastor has said that God's election and our free will are like a set of railroad tracks that, while separated by crossties whenever we view them up close, come together at some point as our eyes follow them to the horizon. While in this life our freedom and God's sovereignty appear to be in conflict in theory, they somehow are wed together in the horizon of eternity.

J. I. Packer likened this matter to an antinomy, with the appearance of contradiction between the two conclusions. According to Packer, "There are cogent reasons for believing each of them; each rests on clear and solid evidence; but it is a mystery to you how they can be squared with each other. You see that each must be true on its own, but you do not see how they can both be true together."[2] He concluded, "Both are thus guaranteed to us by the same divine authority; both, therefore, are true. It follows that they must be held together, and not played off against each other. Man is a responsible moral agent, though he is also divinely controlled; man is divinely controlled, though he is also a responsible moral agent. God's sovereignty is a reality, and man's responsibility is a reality too."[3]

Just as we read several verses related to election and predestination in chapter 10, I want to show you several passages of Scripture related to the desire of God for people to repent and come to him and the universal nature of this invitation.[4]

- "Say to them, As I live, declares the Lord GOD, I have no pleasure in the death of the wicked, but that the wicked turn from his way and live; turn back, turn back from your evil ways, for why will you die, O house of Israel?" (Ezekiel 33:11).
- "To him all the prophets bear witness that everyone who believes in him receives forgiveness of sins through his name" (Acts 10:43).
- "Everyone who calls on the name of the Lord will be saved" (Romans 10:13).

- The Lord is not slow to fulfill his promise as some count slowness, but is patient toward you, not wishing that any should perish, but that all should reach repentance (2 Peter 3:9).

The Extent of the Fall on the Will

The two primary evangelical understandings of free will come from the Wesleyan/Arminian and the Reformed/Calvinist perspectives. Both the Wesleyan/Arminian and the Reformed/Calvinist traditions would agree that it is from Adam that we have received our sin nature, including the tendency to sin. Describing the effects of sin, Paul wrote:

> For we have already charged that all, both Jews and Greeks, are under sin, as it is written: "None is righteous, no, not one; no one understands; no one seeks for God. All have turned aside; together they have become worthless; no one does good, not even one."
>
> "Their throat is an open grave; they use their tongues to deceive."
>
> "The venom of asps is under their lips."
>
> "Their mouth is full of curses and bitterness."
>
> "Their feet are swift to shed blood; in their paths are ruin and misery, and the way of peace they have not known."
>
> "There is no fear of God before their eyes" (Romans 3:9–18).

While each tradition would agree with Paul's words, each understands differently the extent of the effects of the fall on the will and how a person comes to repent and place faith in Jesus.

According to the Wesleyan/Arminian camp, men and women are sinful but have the freedom to choose to follow or reject Jesus. The Wesleyan/Arminian tradition generally holds to the perspective that the effects of the fall were not so extensive that an individual's will has been completely bound. We are separated from God but not so far removed that we are unable to reach out to God as he reaches out to us. As a result of Jesus' death on the cross, the grace of God makes all people capable of responding positively to the gospel. God takes the initiative in that his saving grace is offered to all, but ultimately each of us can make the choice for salvation or resist the grace of God. In other words, we choose God's salvation in conjunction with God's grace, resulting in repentance and faith. God is able to save us only when we choose to accept his good news.

The Reformed/Calvinist tradition argues that because men and women are totally depraved and separated from God, the will is in bondage. The effects of the fall on human will are so extensive that left to our own choosing, we would reject God's good news *every time* it is presented. Fallen people are free to choose as they desire every time, but because their desire is anti-God, they will always refuse the offer. Human will is bound in slavery to sin (John 8:31–38).

The grace of God to the elect, however, breaks the bonds of sin, setting the will free. Whenever anyone is made alive by the Holy Spirit, he repents and places faith in Jesus only because God breaks the chains of bondage, liberating the will. Since God's love and the gospel are so wonderful, the person will then *always* choose to follow Jesus, for the desire is now for God, and the will responds accordingly. Only those willing to follow Jesus experience God's salvation. When God determines to redeem someone, as with everything else God does, his plans are never thwarted by human will. His will is done on earth as it is in heaven. Miraculously, he makes the dead become alive, the blind to see, and the unwilling become willing. As the omnipotent Sovereign, his activity bears fruit.

Some Matters to Keep in Mind

As with the doctrine of election, we must also keep in mind some facts related to human freedom and salvation that must be reflected in our evangelistic work.

We Can Do Nothing to Obtain Salvation

It is only by grace we are saved through faith, with both grace and faith being gifts of God (Ephesians 2:8–9). Nothing we do earns us our salvation. As we noted earlier, even our best deeds before a holy God are like filthy rags compared to his righteousness (Isaiah 64:6).

God Calls All to Repent and Believe the Gospel

The command to come to Jesus is extended to all people, young and old, male and female, wise and foolish, rich and poor. The declaration to place faith in Jesus alone for salvation is extended to all, regardless of nationality, ethnicity, social class, or political views. Whosoever wants to come to Jesus may come, and we must share the invitation this way.

Everyone Who Repents and Places Faith in Jesus Will Be Saved

When it comes to salvation, there is no difference between Jew or Greek, male or female, slave or freeman (Galatians 3:28). God is no respecter of persons. Salvation is provided to those who follow Jesus.

God Holds Us Accountable for Deciding to Reject Jesus

Everyone who rejects the invitation extended by God is personally responsible for that decision. Unless we repent, we will perish (Luke 13:3).

Questions to Consider

- Are you troubled by the fact that the Bible supports both God's sovereignty and our decision to choose or reject Christ? If so, why does this matter cause you concern? Are you troubled by other passages of the Bible that are difficult to explain? Which ones?
- Do you tend to be more Wesleyan/Arminian or Reformed/Calvinist in your understanding of free will and salvation? Can you support your perspective from the Bible?
- Does your view on the freedom of the will affect the way you do evangelism? If so, why? Should it affect your methods?

CHAPTER 13

WHAT ABOUT THOSE WHO NEVER HEAR THE GOSPEL?

"Then what about the man on the remote island somewhere?" Mark asked.

"Who?"

"Well, we've been talking about free will and salvation and the fact that the call to repent and follow Jesus goes out to people and the elect come to faith in Jesus. But you know, the man alone on an isolated island or in the deepest, darkest Amazonian jungle, or someplace else where he never has a chance to hear the gospel—what happens to him?"

"Oh, I'm sure by now they've discovered all the Amazonian peoples," Roberto chided, "and there are no remote islands anymore with all the satellites up there. Why, I just heard the other day that you can be anywhere on the planet in forty-eight hours."

"Dude! You know what I mean. What happens to the man who lives his life without ever hearing the gospel, due to something like geographical location? Does he go to hell?"

"I know what you're talking about. I'm just aggravating you. Well, let's talk about that. What do we know so far?"

Mark reflected on the evening's intensive conversation. "OK—we are all sinners against a holy God. Because of this fact, fairness and justice mean that we're dead spiritually and deserve hell. However, while we were yet sinners, Christ died for us. Prior to the creation of the world, God in his foreknowledge decided to extend grace and mercy to some people, by predestining them for salvation. These people are the elect. Some theologians believe that God looked down the corridors of time and elected those he foreknew would repent and place their faith in Christ. Others believe that God elected them not because of anything they did—for they were spiritually dead and could not respond on their own—but simply out of his sovereign will. . . . So far, so good?"

Roberto nodded. "And whether someone is Wesleyan/Arminian or Reformed/Calvinist, the proclamation of the good news is the power of God to save."

"So what about the isolated dude, Roberto?"

//

Mark's question about the hypothetical man on an island miles from civilization is a question that many have asked. The simple answer is that unless a person turns from sin and places explicit faith in Christ, there is no salvation. Jesus said, "I am the way, and the truth, and the life. No one comes to the Father except through me" (John 14:6). Even while speaking to very religious men, Peter and John stated, "There is salvation in no one else, for there is no other name under heaven given among men by which we must be saved" (Acts 4:12).

So what does this matter teach us? First, it reveals to the church the *responsibility* to take the gospel to the ends of the earth, just as Jesus commanded us long ago. If there is one unbeliever present on some remote island, we are to go and share.

Second, it reminds the church of the *urgency* to take the gospel to the unreached. A story was once told of a remote people who embraced the gospel, only to ask the missionaries, "What took you so long to get here to tell our people about this great truth?" Regardless of our belief concerning election, our love for lost people should cause us to want unbelievers to come to faith sooner rather than later. We should want to see them free from the bondage of the evil one and growing in the blessings of Christ.

Third, while Mark asked a hypothetical question, the fact is such people do exist. While not always on some remote island, as of the time of this writing there are still numerous people groups who do not have anyone explaining the gospel to them. Mark's question challenges us to be people traveling the globe searching for those who have not been engaged with the truth. The apostle Paul is a good model for us in light of Mark's question. Paul told Timothy, "Therefore I endure everything for the sake of the elect, that they also may obtain the salvation that is in Christ Jesus with eternal glory" (2 Timothy 2:10).

Differing Views on the Fate of the Unevangelized

The following are differing views related to the salvation of those who never have a chance to hear the gospel. The first on the list is the only view that has substantial scriptural evidence for support.

- Exclusivism. Jesus is the only way of salvation, and explicit faith must be placed in him.
- Inclusivism. Jesus is the only way of salvation, but people can come to the Father without knowledge of Jesus through sincerity in other religions and faith traditions. They are simply anonymous Christians, resting unknowingly in Jesus' atoning sacrifice on the cross.
- Pluralism. Jesus is not the only Savior, and there are many ways of salvation.
- Universalism. Everyone will be saved ultimately.
- Postmortem evangelization (divine perseverance). Some people will be offered a chance to receive Jesus after death.
- Middle knowledge. God may extend salvation to those who die without hearing the gospel if he knows that they would have believed in Jesus if they had heard the gospel.
- Final option theory. This is similar to the postmortem evangelization perspective. Some Roman Catholics advocate that at the moment of death (but not after death), a person encounters Christ, who provides an opportunity to be saved.
- Agnostic. God will save the vast majority of the human race, but we simply do not know how he will do it when it comes to the unevangelized.
- Negative agnostic. God might provide a way of salvation to some of the unevangelized, but we have no reason to think he will.[1]

The Cornelius Factor

A response to Mark's question needs to take into consideration what I call the Cornelius factor. In Acts 10, Cornelius is noted as a significant military leader, but he was not a follower of Jesus. Rather, Luke describes him as "a devout man who feared God with all his household." A God fearer? Yes. A forgiven and saved man? No. Remember, we are not saved by our deeds or by believing in God and fearing him (Ephesians 2:8–9; James 2:19). Yet in Cornelius's search for truth, God revealed to him what he was to do—invite the apostle Peter to his house (Acts 10:5). It was only after Peter arrived and shared the gospel with Cornelius that his entire household came to faith in Christ (vv. 34–48).

The Bible teaches that "the heavens declare the glory of God, and the sky above proclaims his handiwork" (Psalm 19:1), and that such knowledge of a divine Creator is understood by everyone (Romans 1:19–20), even the man on the island. However, this natural revelation of God's grace is not sufficient for anyone to come to faith in him. Paul commented on this matter:

> For the wrath of God is revealed from heaven against all ungodliness and unrighteousness of men, who by their unrighteousness suppress the truth. For what can be known about God is plain to them, because God has shown it to them. For his invisible attributes, namely, his eternal power and divine nature, have been clearly perceived, ever since the creation of the world, in the things that have been made. So they are without excuse. For although they knew God, they did not honor him as God or give thanks to him, but they became futile in their thinking, and their foolish hearts were darkened. Claiming to be wise, they became fools, and exchanged the glory of the immortal God for images resembling mortal man and birds and animals and creeping things.
>
> Therefore God gave them up in the lusts of their hearts to impurity, to the dishonoring of their bodies among themselves, because they exchanged the truth about God for a lie and worshiped and served the creature rather than the Creator, who is blessed forever! Amen (Romans 1:18–25).

What does this have to do with Mark's question about the man on the island? To use a metaphor from the art world, the Grand Artist has painted on the canvas of the universe and the hearts of all people to reveal his glory. However, because of our sinful hearts, we suppress this truth that we know about God. Instead of responding positively to God's glory revealed through his wondrous creation and our own consciences, we refuse to thank him and worship him for who he is but begin to worship the creation, including ourselves. Creation becomes an idol in place of the Creator. The result is that we go our own way apart from God; and God allows us to have it our own way.

So while the man on the island is able to see the same sun, moon, stars, rain, and animals that Mark and Roberto are able to see, like everyone else he will turn away from the Creator of these marvelous things. He will live by his own rules in his social context apart from the God who created him and loves him.

Having read the previous chapters, you might now be asking, "Is the man on the island one of the elect?" If that is the case, then you are asking the wrong question. Again, the church is not called to be a Sherlock Holmes, attempting to figure out the mysteries of God. Rather, we are commanded to go, to love, and to proclaim the gospel to everyone whether across the street or on the most remote island.

Remember, the Cornelius factor advocates that God is a missionary working among the people in the world but requires that his church take the good news of Jesus even to the religiously devout. Just as God worked in a miraculous way to lead Peter to Cornelius's house, he still works in such ways to lead his people to the man on the island. While Cornelius was not geographically separated from Peter on some remote island, in relationship to Peter he was on a social island. Peter was Jewish and would not even spell *Gentile* for fear of becoming unclean, and Cornelius was a Gentile. God had to give Peter a vision and speak to him directly to release Peter from his traditional fears of socializing with people of other races.

What we *can* say about the man on the island is that he has the ability to respond to the gospel if someone presents it to him in a way he can understand. I cannot tell you whether he will embrace Christ. Only God knows. The church has a mandate to find him, love him, and share the message of hope, regardless of his response. However, unless there is belief in the person of Jesus, the man will perish (John 3:16).

Questions to Consider

- Of the differing views on the fate of the unevangelized, with which perspective do you agree? Can you find biblical support for your conviction?
- Does the thought of the man on the island without Christ trouble you? Does it trouble you enough to go and share the gospel with him?

CHAPTER 14

WHAT ABOUT CHILDREN WHO DIE AND THE MENTALLY DISABLED?

"So now I have a question for you, Mark. What do you think about the salvation of those who die before hearing the gospel, who are not geographically isolated like the man on the island?" Roberto asked.

"Like who? I'm not following you."

"Well, like children who die or those who are mentally disabled," Roberto clarified.

Mark sighed deeply. "Well, I've never thought about that before. I guess there seems to be a difference between the man on the island and children who die or the mentally incapacitated."

"Like what?"

"Well, they can't . . . respond."

"Go on," Roberto said. "You're on a good path."

"They don't have the ability to respond even if someone explained the gospel to them. I think I remember several places in the Scriptures that might apply to this question."

"Do you remember where the passages are found?" Roberto asked.

"Maybe," Mark said. "I probably can find them if you help me."

//

Roberto and Mark have tackled another challenging question, and like the man-on-the-island question, this one has been asked for centuries—particularly related to the death of children. This is a very good question that most of us can relate to, as opposed to the man-on-the-island question. As with all the questions in this book, we must make certain we look for biblical responses.

Typical responses related to the salvation of children who die without hearing the gospel and the mentally disabled who cannot respond include the following:

- Emotional response. God is love, and children (and mentally incapacitated people) are innocent creatures. Therefore, there is no way that such people should spend eternity in hell.
- Without hope response. There is no hope for children who die in infancy or for the disabled who are incapable of responding to the gospel. Since they did not repent and place faith in Jesus, they will spend eternity in hell.
- Elect response. All children and mentally disabled people who die without having an opportunity to hear and respond to the gospel are of the elect.
- Variation on the elect response. It is unknown whether children or the mentally disabled are of the elect. If they are of the elect, they will be in heaven. If they are not of the elect, they will be in hell.
- Church-tradition response. If children or the mentally disabled are baptized and part of a believing family, they will go to heaven. Some find support in this perspective from 1 Corinthians 7:14.[1]
- Postmortem evangelization response. Those who have not been able or never had a chance to respond to the gospel will be offered an opportunity following death and before entering heaven or hell.

The Bible does not have a great deal to say about this issue, but there are some passages that I believe will assist us in our thinking.

First, we must understand that those who die in infancy and mentally disabled people are born into sin just like the rest of humanity (Romans 5:12). Jesus is the only Savior who provides atonement (John 14:6; Acts 4:12), and God is sovereign in electing people to salvation (Ephesians 1:4–5).

Second, sinners are held accountable for all their deeds (Revelation 20:11–15). I believe we can find hope in the assumption that children and the disabled who die, having no understanding of right or wrong, are not held accountable for any wrong deeds (Deuteronomy 1:34–39).

Third, Jesus clearly has a special place in his heart for children (Matthew 18:1–6; 19:14; Mark 10:13–16). Some have argued that those "who do not know their right hand from their left" (Jonah 4:11) were the children in Nineveh, thus revealing the object of God's compassion.

Fourth, some have argued that when David acknowledged that he would go to the place of his dead child (2 Samuel 2:23) he was referring to heaven, because he knew that he was going to heaven.[2]

Fifth, as Mark mentioned to Roberto, another matter to consider in relation to this question is that of the *capacity* of the child or mentally disabled person to respond to the gospel. In other words, unlike the man on the island in chapter 13, these individuals *would not be able* to repent and place faith in Jesus even if they were presented the clearest plan of salvation before their death. They have no capability to comprehend or understand such truth or to respond in faith. For we must remember that faith comes by being able to grasp the Word (Romans 10:17).

The fate of children and those with mental disabilities is not an easy question to answer, but one that we must address. Some of our excellent questions are not answered as clearly and as thoroughly as we would like. We must rest assured, however, that the Lord has provided us in Scripture with the answers that we need. Where the Scriptures shout answers aloud, we are free to cry out. Where the Scriptures whisper, we must speak softly. And where the Scriptures are silent, we must hold our tongue. Regardless of our response, we are to know that God is an all-good, compassionate, loving, gracious, merciful, kind, just, and saving Lord who cares more about the death and salvation of children and mentally disabled people than you or I ever will.

Questions to Consider

- Of the different ways people typically respond to the question of this chapter, which one best describes you? Why? Can you support your position from the Scriptures?

- Do you agree or disagree with the contrasting situations of the man on the island and that of children and those who are mentally disabled? Why?

CHAPTER 15

WHAT IS THE HOLY SPIRIT'S ROLE IN EVANGELISM?

With final exams only a few days away, tonight's meeting would steal time from study time, but Mark recognized he needed a break and a blessing. And tonight he actually got to Beans before Roberto arrived.

"Running late," Roberto said. "Needed an oil change and didn't think it would take so long." After getting their orders, they located a small table in a back corner. "It's busy tonight."

"I wish they would sell stock in this joint. I would be the first in line!" Mark replied.

Roberto sipped his coffee. "Mark, while I was getting my oil changed tonight, I was thinking."

"Wow! You *think*?" Mark joked.

But Roberto acted as if he hadn't heard. "Bro, why do you think there is such little mention of the Holy Spirit in the Christian life?"

Mark shrugged and took a bite of his cheesecake.

"I don't think believers today spend much time talking about the work of the Holy Spirit," Roberto added. "But maybe I'm just out of touch with what is going on."

"Well, now that I think about it, I don't recall hearing much discussion or teaching on the Holy Spirit for some time," Mark said. "It's almost like he's the forgotten person of the Trinity."

"Forgotten but absolutely necessary, especially concerning evangelism!" Roberto said. "You know, I can probably think of a few reasons why that might be true."

"Like what?"

"Well, for starters, familiarity breeds contempt," Roberto said. "I remember my childhood visits with my grandfather. He lived beside a railroad track—I mean right beside the thing, fifty feet from his living room! Whenever a train came along, it shook the entire house! Loud? You'd better believe it! On any given day, five trains passed by his place."

"OK? What's the point?" Mark wondered if Roberto had lost focus.

"The point is that he got used to living there. He had heard the trains for so long that after six years in that house, he never *heard* them. Every time I would visit and heard the first train pass, I would ask my grandfather how in the world he could live here with all that noise. Several times he responded that he hadn't noticed a train had gone by! I thought the dude was crazy. But he had become so accustomed to the trains that he learned to ignore them. I think we take the Spirit for granted too and simply forget about him."

"Great point," Mark commented, sipping his espresso. "What else?"

"Well, I think we are ignorant about the biblical teachings regarding the Spirit. We simply don't know what the Bible says about his character and work. I also believe that many evangelicals are afraid that if they spend too much time talking about the Holy Spirit that they will be labeled extremists, and they don't want that. Also there's been a great deal of false teaching about the Holy Spirit that has caused some people to avoid the subject. They have witnessed so much extremism and abuse of the doctrine of the Spirit that they have reacted in a negative way."

"I can see that," Mark said.

"Mark, maybe the Spirit is leading us to spend some of our time discussing his involvement in our witnessing. What is this Spirit's work in evangelism?"

Mark thought for a moment. "Well, I can think of a few biblical passages that help answer your question. Can we take a look at them?"

"Sure," Roberto said, and he pushed his Bible across the table to Mark.

//

Millard J. Erickson was correct when he wrote, "If we are to be in touch with God today, then, we must become acquainted with the Holy Sprit's activity."[1] There is no place for contempt, ignorance, or ungodly fear when it comes to knowing the Lord. In order for us to continue to grow in our walk with him, we must better understand him and his ways. Any discussion of evangelism must include the work of the third person of the Trinity. Without the Spirit, all efforts to advance the kingdom are in vain. Let's take a look at a few of the ways the Spirit works through the missional labors of the church.

Power

The Spirit of God is omnipotent (all-powerful), and this divine power is revealed throughout the Scriptures. Jesus was empowered by the Spirit for his earthly ministry (Luke 4:14–21). After his resurrection, Jesus told the apostles to wait in Jerusalem until they received the Holy Spirit, who would empower them for their ministry of preaching the gospel to the ends of the earth (Acts 1:1–8). The Spirit enabled the church to bear a powerful witness to the resurrection of Jesus, and the Lord expanded his kingdom through their testimony, as we see throughout the book of Acts.

In his letters to the churches in Rome, Ephesus, and Galatia, Paul often commented on the power of the Spirit, for example, in Romans 15:13, Ephesians 3:16, and Galatians 4:29. It is this empowerment that enables us today to accomplish more for Christ's glory than we could imagine or ask: "Now to him who is able to do far more abundantly than all that we ask or think, according to the power at work within us, to him be glory in the church and in Christ Jesus throughout all generations, forever and ever" (Ephesians 3:20–21).

Guidance

We must rely on the Spirit to guide our steps and interactions with others each day. In the book of Acts, we see him at work providing such guidance. For example, after the great awakening in Samaria, the Spirit led Philip into the desert to explain the gospel to a very receptive Ethiopian (Acts 8:26–38). The Spirit also guided the church-planting team away from Asia Minor and Bithynia but toward Philippi to preach and plant a church (Acts 16).

Boldness

The boldness for proclaiming a message that is foolishness to the world comes from the Spirit. When the first church faced opposition, they prayed for boldness to evangelize, and the Spirit supplied this power: "'And now, Lord, look upon their threats and grant to your servants to continue to speak your word with all boldness. . . .' And when they had prayed, the place in which they were gathered together was shaken, and they were all filled with the Holy Spirit and continued to speak the word of God with boldness" (Acts 4:29, 31).

Wisdom

It was the Spirit who, when the disciples were arrested for preaching the gospel, spoke through Peter and John (although they were uneducated) and also through Stephen, confounding the religious leaders (Acts 4:13; 6:10). These instances were fulfillments of Jesus' teaching: "And when they bring you to trial and deliver you over, do not be anxious beforehand what you are to say, but say whatever is given you in that hour, for it is not you who speak, but the Holy Spirit" (Mark 13:11).

God's Glory

From Genesis to Revelation, the Spirit is shown continually working out his will in the world for God's glory. He is at work in the lives of people before we arrive to tell them the good news, and he will continue to work long after we are gone. Remember, in Samaria Jesus told his disciples that as they went out to minister, sometimes they would reap the harvest of those who had labored before them and planted seeds that grew (John 4:34–38).

Conviction

J. B. Lawrence correctly wrote, "Human instruments, apart from the Holy Spirit, cannot change dead hearts, obstinate wills, evil imaginations, perverted understanding, and biased judgments."[2] It is the Spirit who works through the gospel to bring to people's attention their separation from a holy God and the greatness of his grace through Jesus. Our evangelism is not with persuasive words but rather the Spirit's power (1 Corinthians 2:4; 1 Thessalonians 1:5; 1 Peter 1:12). The Spirit convicts people of sin and convinces them of the righteousness and judgment of God (John 16:8).

Salvation

We cannot save a person no matter how hard we try. This glory belongs to the Spirit (John 3:5–8; Acts 16:14; 1 Corinthians 12:3). He loves the unbeliever more than we do. We must make certain that we never attempt to rob God of his job by manipulating or coercing someone to make a false profession of faith in Jesus. God is not lazy, needing you or me to save someone. Nor will he idly stand by and be robbed of his glory! John Stott made an excellent point regarding the Spirit and the unbeliever when he wrote, "Only the Holy Spirit can open his eyes, enlighten his darkness, liberate him from bondage, turn him to God and bring him out of death into life."[3]

Questions to Consider

- Of all of the ways the Spirit is involved in evangelism, which one provides you with the most encouragement for witnessing? Why?
- Have you been too self-sufficient in your witnessing and not relied on the Spirit? If so, what can you now do to correct this?

CHAPTER 16

WHAT IS THE ROLE OF
PRAYER IN EVANGELISM?

After discussing with Roberto the relationship of the Spirit to evange-lism, Mark wanted to raise another question before they ran out of time. He knew Roberto had to return home earlier than usual to help his family get ready for relatives coming for Thanksgiving. "Since we only have a few minutes left tonight, I want to bring up another question," Mark said. "How about prayer and evangelism?"

"Can you explain?"

"You mentioned that you were going to pray for the dude who changed your oil tonight. You said that when you were in the garage tonight, you were praying for an opportunity to talk with him about Jesus, but the situa-tion didn't allow any such discussion."

"Or any discussion, for that matter," Roberto said.

"We've already talked about the fact that God is sovereign in evangelism. But where does prayer fit in?" Mark asked.

"You mean if God is in control of everything, then why do we even pray when it comes to someone's salvation?"

"Yeah! I think that's an interesting question."

"I think so too," Roberto replied.

"That's why they pay me the big bucks!" Mark declared.

//

Just as the Lord has ordained to save the elect through the preaching of the gospel, the Lord has also ordained prayer to be part of the process of them coming to faith. We know that prayer is not simply the means for us to get things from God, as if he were a giant vending machine dispensing what we want at the push of a button. We understand that as we spend time with our Father in prayer and express to him our deepest feelings and thoughts, he increases our faith. And when it comes to evangelism, the sovereign Lord again works in and through our prayers to accomplish his good purposes.

Daily Prayer

All evangelicals pray that God will save people. We all pray for God to save our friends, family members, and total strangers. There are at least eight scriptural teachings that should guide us regarding the place of prayer in evangelism. The first four of these relate to daily prayer.

God's Will Be Done

While the faithful and intense prayer of a righteous person is powerful (James 5:16), the sovereign Lord of the universe is not simply a puppet on a string that we can manipulate according to our desires, even seemingly good desires. We cannot manipulate him by doing the right things, making the proper sacrifices, or speaking the correct prayers.

Whenever we pray, we must always remember the words of Jesus in his model prayer: "Your kingdom come, your will be done, on earth as it is in heaven" (Matthew 6:10). We pray in accordance with the will of God on earth. I remember praying for years for the salvation of someone, only to never see him place his belief in Jesus before his death. Was I saddened by the fact that to my knowledge this person missed the abundant life that only Jesus provides? Yes! Was I upset by the fact that this individual by all appearances may not have entered into heaven? Yes! Was my faith in the power of God to work through prayer to bring people into the kingdom shaken? Absolutely not! I know that the Lord hears the prayers of the righteous (1 Peter 3:12). He is God and loves his creation more than I do. He is sovereign, and as his servant, I simply cry out, "Your will be done, on earth as it is in heaven."

Pray Believing

Another important part of prayer is that we pray believing that the Lord will work. Mark wrote, "Therefore I tell you, whatever you ask in prayer, believe that you have received it, and it will be yours" (Mark 11:24). This passage is not some name-it-and-claim-it ticket to get whatever we want. Rather, we pray believing that the Lord of the harvest is capable, able, and will bring some of the wicked sinners into his kingdom.

I clearly remember Kevin, a teenager I met one week when I served as a summer camp pastor. Kevin was one bad dude. In fact, I think I got an ulcer that week because of him. He was the most disobedient kid of the entire summer. The only time he was not causing trouble was when he was sleeping. I thought the camp director was going to have to call his parents and send him home.

I remember praying hard for Kevin that week. I prayed for two things: that he would not kill anyone and that he would come to follow Jesus. Everyone was praying for him. And to make a long story of a very rough week short, the Lord graciously brought Kevin into the kingdom that week at camp.

On his last day at camp, shortly before he left, Kevin walked over to me, took out a bracelet he had made during craft time, and proceeded to tie it onto my wrist. Since every time I got near this kid all week I had tensed all my abs, fearing a punch in the stomach, I instinctively braced myself for a sucker punch. (He may have been a believer for twenty-four hours, but I know that complete sanctification doesn't happen overnight!) While I was thinking that he was going to use the bracelet as a tourniquet and cut off the blood flow to my hand, I quickly realized that his demeanor was changed.

"Do you know what that bracelet means?" he asked. "That means thank-you for praying for me."

While I spent only a few days praying for Kevin, I have spent over sixteen years praying for family members who still are not followers of Jesus. The point is that when we pray for the salvation of others, we pray believing in God to work.

Do Not Lose Heart

Whenever we pray to the Lord of the harvest (Luke 10:2), we should do so without becoming discouraged. Sometimes when the Lord is not answering our prayers in the way we desire and in our time frame, we lose heart, but Jesus taught his disciples that "they ought always to pray and not lose heart"

(Luke 18:1). We should not grow weary in praying for the salvation of others and for opportunities to share the truth with them.

Pray at All Times

On at least two occasions, Paul wrote to believers that they should pray at all times (Ephesians 6:18; 1 Thessalonians 5:17). While these commands are elements of the life of being on a journey with Jesus, they apply to evangelism as well. We should be praying for the salvation of others as we meet them each day while on life's daily venture.

Prayer in Evangelism

The next four teachings on prayer should specifically guide our prayer times when it comes to evangelism.

Pray for Boldness

Paul, writing to the Ephesian believers, asked them to pray for him so that he would have the correct words to speak and for boldness (Ephesians 6:18–20). I have never experienced such persecution for my faith as Paul did, but I *often* lack boldness. Yet many times I have prayed for boldness to speak and the Lord melted away my intimidation and allowed the witnessing time to feel like a very natural conversation.

Pray for the Spread of the Gospel

As followers of Jesus, we should also pray that the gospel would quickly spread from person to person and that it would be honored as it spreads. Paul made this request to the Thessalonian believers (2 Thessalonians 3:1). It is important that the gospel be rapidly disseminated across a people group or population segment and that people come to place their faith in Jesus.

Pray for Salvation

Whether we are from the Wesleyan/Arminian camp or from the Reformed/Calvinist camp, we all must cry out to the sovereign Lord to bring about the salvation of souls. Paul had a great desire to see his people, Israel, come to faith in Jesus, and he acted on that desire by interceding for their salvation (Romans 10:1).

Pray for Opportunities

We should pray for opportunities to share the gospel with others (Colossians 4:3).

Each day for the past several years, during my devotional time with the Lord, I have asked for opportunities to share the good news with others during that day. The Lord has many times opened such doors for me. Sometimes I have been faithful to walk through those doors, and sometimes I have not. Sometimes I have been able to share with a stranger, sometimes a family member, friend, or neighbor. Sometimes the Lord brought Mormons or Jehovah's Witnesses to my door to hear the gospel.

We should pray for daily opportunities and then walk through our day with "evangelistic eyes" open to the opportunities God provides.

Questions to Consider

- Of these eight different matters related to prayer, which do you need to add to your regular times of prayer?
- Does it seem strange to you that the Scriptures teach that God is sovereign in all matters but that we should be involved in praying for the salvation of others? If your answer is yes, explain your thinking.

CHAPTER 17

IS THERE A GIFT OF EVANGELISM?

As always, Mark was looking forward to his meeting with Roberto. This time he was eager to tell him about a conversation with his cousin Sam over the Thanksgiving holiday. Sam was a believer and held many of the same convictions as Mark. But when their conversation turned to the topic of sharing the gospel with others, Sam was not such a kindred spirit.

After ordering his usual, Mark sat down with Roberto. "Interesting encounter I had this past week."

"Let's hear it," Roberto said.

"I was talking with one of my relatives who lives in Philly. I told him about our weekly conversations and how we've been talking about evangelism lately. Well, told me that he is not very intentional about sharing his faith on a regular basis because he believes evangelism is mainly for those with the gift of evangelism. He said he once took a spiritual gifts test and learned he doesn't have the gift of evangelism."

"Hmm," said Roberto. He blew across the top of his mug to cool his coffee. "Interesting. Let's talk about this. I've heard that argument before, but it's not a strong case for not doing evangelism."

"All I know is that I don't have it," Mark declared.

"Have what?" Roberto asked with concern in his voice.

"The gift of evangelism—I don't have it."

"Who told you there is a gift of evangelism?"

"Well, the spiritual gifts inventory we took at church last year listed evangelism as a gift—and I didn't have it."

"Mark," Roberto said brusquely. "Two things: first, those surveys are a modern instrument sometimes applying contemporary definitions to first-century concepts. So we must take the findings of such modern tools with a grain of salt. The best way to understand our giftedness is through service in the body of Christ. We must hear from the Spirit and other brothers and sisters about our possible giftedness as we serve. Second, there is no clear passage of Scripture that states there is a gift of evangelism."

"What about that passage that says Jesus gave to his church pastors, apostles, and evangelists, and some other gifts?" Mark asked.

"Good memory to recall Ephesians 4," Roberto said. He opened his Bible. "Here, let's take a look at it."

//

Over the years, I have heard many people refer to the gift of evangelism. I have seen evangelism listed on spiritual gifts inventories, and I have found myself (and many others) scoring high in the area of evangelism, meaning, in terms of the test, that we "have the gift."

But is there such a gift? Are gift inventories definitive, indicating who has and does not have certain gifts? When we examine the Scriptures, we find that there is no place in the Bible where a gift of evangelism is mentioned. In the major lists of spiritual gifts, evangelism is not one of the gifts (Romans 12:3–8; 1 Corinthians 12; 14; 1 Peter 4:10–11).

What *do* the Scriptures say? The word *evangelist* is used three times in the Bible. Luke referred to Philip as an evangelist in Acts 21:28, and Paul used the word twice. First, he noted that the Lord "gave the apostles, the prophets, the evangelists, the shepherds and teachers, to equip the saints for the work of ministry, for building up the body of Christ" (Ephesians 4:11–12). He also wrote to Timothy, reminding him to "always be sober-minded, endure suffering, do the work of an evangelist, fulfill your ministry" (2 Timothy 4:5).

What are we to make from these references?

The Gift to the Church Was Leadership

Again, we note that in the passage in Ephesians Christ gave evangelists to the early church for ministry in building up the body of Christ. While it is clear that evangelists were a gift to the church, we cannot deduce from this passage that there is a gift of evangelism any more than we can deduce that there are gifts of pastoring and "apostling."

Granted, there are gifts of prophecy and teaching clearly listed in other passages. So based on this evidence, while it might be possible that unnamed gifts of "apostling," pastoring, and evangelism exist, to be fair, the gifts of prophecy and teaching are also listed in the same verses as other gifts for which there is no clear biblical office (for example, serving, exhorting, and giving).

I do agree that if there is a gift of evangelism, the evangelist would be the person most likely endowed with that gift. But such thinking, while interesting, is speculation. While there is clear evidence for the gift of the evangelist, there simply is not enough information from the Bible to make a strong case for the gift of evangelism.

So from Ephesians 4:11–12, we come to understand that a major responsibility of the evangelist was to prepare followers of Jesus for growing the church. While there were probably many evangelists, Philip is the only one mentioned by name (Acts 21:28). If Philip's actions were representative of all the evangelists, we know from Acts 8 that they were involved in evangelism and church planting.

Missionary Work Involves Evangelism

Paul reminded Timothy to set things in order in the church at Ephesus and teach faithful men to pass along the truths to others (2 Timothy 2:2). The church at Ephesus already had elders in place (Acts 20:17); Timothy was not a permanent pastoral fixture there but was completing work that had been left undone. Paul urged him to work as an evangelist while in Ephesus (2 Timothy 4:5). This would obviously involve the preaching of the good news to unbelievers and equipping the church for the work of the ministry.

All Believers Should Share the Gospel

Every believer is to be involved in sharing the gospel, regardless of giftedness. While not everyone is called to be an evangelist—just like not everyone is called to be an apostle, prophet, or pastor-teacher—one thing is very clear: everyone in the body of Christ is to be involved in telling others of the risen Savior. We are brought into God's family to be a blessing to others (Genesis 12:1–3), to make disciples of all nations (Matthew 28:19), to preach repentance and forgiveness (Luke 24:47), to be a witness for him (Acts 1:8), and to proclaim his glories (1 Peter 2:9).

What If I Am Wrong?

Let's look at this another way. Let's say that I'm wrong and there is a gift of evangelism. Would this truth allow us to respond like Mark's relative or the guys in Mark's church?

When I was in seminary, I had a professor who told the class that every time he took a spiritual gifts inventory he scored a zero for the gift of mercy. Now, before you form a negative opinion of this man, you need to know the rest of the story. While he might not have had the gift of mercy (assuming the gifts assessment was accurate), he recognized that as a follower of Jesus, he was called to be merciful; and he was merciful.

If the gift of evangelism exists but we do not have the gift, would we then be excused for not being intentional about sharing the gospel with others? Of course not! As followers of Jesus, can we say that we are exempt from giving because we don't have the spiritual gift of giving? Or can we escape from helping, simply because the Spirit has not graced us with this gift either? Of course not! Not everyone is called to lead as a pastor, but there will be times when all of us shepherd and teach other brothers and sisters so they can grow in Christ. In the same way, as we take advantage of opportunities to tell others about Christ, the Holy Spirit will enable us to witness effectively.

Questions to Consider
- Do you believe that there is a special gift of evangelism? Can you support your belief from Scripture?
- How does your belief about a gift of evangelism affect your personal witness?

CHAPTER 18
WHAT IS LIFESTYLE EVANGELISM?

"OK, so since you just put the smackdown on my cousin and his understanding of spiritual gifts—"

"I did not put the smackdown on him," Roberto declared with a light-hearted smile. "Just a slight rebuke."

"Whatever," Mark replied. "Anyway, since we are talking about other people tonight, I have another situation for you."

"Don't say we're talking about other people as if we are gossiping or something," Roberto said.

"OK. So here's another one for you," Mark said. "I recently ran into a guy from one of my classes who said he is a Christian but doesn't like me talking to others about Jesus because—he says—it offends people. He said that he practices—"

"I know, lifestyle evangelism."

"Yes! That's it. What is that?"

"Depends on who you're talking to," said Roberto. "For some people, lifestyle evangelism involves everything believers do to share the gospel. For others it's the concept that if we live a good life before others, one day people will ask why we live like we do and then we can explain the gospel. Some believers take it to another extreme and say that living a good Christian life before others is a sufficient witness to the world, without ever explaining the gospel. It sounds to me as if this guy is the type of believer who doesn't like to talk with others about the gospel."

"But if it is evangelism, then by definition doesn't it have to include the communication of the good news?"

"You'd think so. But some people define evangelism as simply 'presence'—just living the right life before others—without saying anything," Roberto replied.

Mark responded with some hesitation in his voice. "Living a good lifestyle doesn't sound so bad. After all, didn't Jesus say in Matthew 5:16, 'Let your light shine before others, so that they may see your good works and give glory to your Father who is in heaven'? I mean, I can kind of see this guy's point. He doesn't want to cause trouble and wants to live a legit life before others. Yet I realize that what he said to me somehow does not sound right. . . . I'm a little confused. Also, didn't Peter write somewhere about being prepared to give a reason for the hope that we have? And I think he also wrote something to wives who were married to unbelieving husbands about living a good life so that their husbands could come to the Lord."

Roberto sensed Mark's frustration. "Well, let's talk about lifestyle evangelism and what the Bible has to say about it," he said calmly.

//

Mark found himself in a situation in which a fellow classmate polarized evangelism as being *either* living a good life before those who are not Jesus' followers *or* verbally telling other people about Jesus. However, the Bible paints a different portrait of evangelism, revealing that one cannot occur without the other. The message and the messenger are tightly connected, and our actions and attitudes affect the way the message is communicated.

The lifestyle of Jesus' followers is very important. Jesus said that not everyone who says, "Lord, Lord" will enter into heaven, but only those who do the will of God (Matthew 7:21). Paul noted that just as we have received Jesus as Lord, we should "walk in him" (Colossians 2:6). Saying we follow Jesus but denying him with our life makes us hypocrites. Living a godly life before unbelievers is a very important component of our evangelism. People today, more so than past generations, want to know we are genuine, if what we claim to be true is actually guiding our lives. They are tired of hearing religious leaders who say one thing and do another.

However, some have distorted the notion of lifestyle evangelism, saying that living a good life before others is sufficient to bring people into the kingdom of God or that we need only live a good life for others to eventually ask us about our faith. Like Mark, some will ask, "But didn't Jesus say to let our light shine before others so that they may see our good works and give glory to God? So I'm going to live a Christlike life before others so they will ask me, 'What makes you different?' and then I will tell them about Jesus." But there are at least three problems with understanding evangelism as simply living a good life that others will see.

Often There Is Not Enough Time

An examination of the Bible reveals many situations in which no time was available for the follower of Jesus to be able to extensively model the Christian life before others. Examples of this are scattered throughout the book of Acts: Philip shared the gospel with the Ethiopian when he first met him (Acts 8:26–40). Upon meeting Cornelius, Peter shared the gospel with him and his household (Acts 10). Many times the apostle Paul and his church-planting teams were in cities only for a short period of time. They preached the gospel to whoever would listen, instead of waiting for people to notice their good lives and ask questions.

In verses we have looked at earlier in this book, Paul wrote to the Roman believers, "How then will they call on him in whom they have not believed? And how are they to believe in him of whom they have never heard? And how are they to hear without someone preaching?" These verses reveal the importance of someone telling the good news to others. And Paul noted that faith comes to the unbeliever by hearing the truth about Jesus (Romans 10:14–17).

Jesus Used Words

A second problem with the "no words" understanding of lifestyle evangelism is that Jesus did not practice such a way of life. We always see Jesus wedding his good behavior that glorified God with his words calling for repentance and believing the good news. Just one of a multitude of examples can be found near the beginning of Mark's Gospel. Jesus was involved in preaching—verbalizing the good news—and casting out demons—helping others in need (Mark 1:39). If anyone could live a perfect lifestyle before others without having to say a word about the gospel, clearly it would have been the one without any sin. Yet even Jesus—who did good deeds to the point of death—also verbalized the gospel (and sometimes offended others when he did).

People Don't Always Ask

A third reason that a "no-words" understanding of lifestyle evangelism is unhealthy for the advancement of the kingdom is simply that some people will never ask, Why are you different? or What do you believe? Over the years I have found this to be true in my own life—most people *never* get around to asking me such questions.

But what about those verses Mark mentioned, the apostle Peter's admonitions to always be prepared to speak when asked and for wives to live a godly life before their unbelieving husbands?

In Peter's first letter we read, "But in your hearts honor Christ the Lord as holy, always being prepared to make a defense to anyone who asks you for a reason for the hope that is in you; yet do it with gentleness and respect, having a good conscience, so that, when you are slandered, those who revile your good behavior in Christ may be put to shame" (1 Peter 3:15–16). Is Peter telling us to keep silent and not speak about Jesus, unless asked? Clearly not. We must keep in mind that we have the whole Bible to assist us in understanding its teachings. In other words, as we have already seen in this chapter, other biblical passages note that we must communicate the gospel with more than good behavior.

Also we must understand the context in which Peter was writing. Those he addressed were or would be experiencing persecution for their faith. At the point of chapter 3, Peter was telling his readers to always be ready to share the hope they had in Christ, even in the days of strong opposition (v. 14).

Peter also wrote, "Likewise, wives, be subject to your own husbands, so that even if some do not obey the word, they may be won without a word by the conduct of their wives, when they see your respectful and pure conduct" (1 Peter 3:1–2). Again, remembering context and that just a few verses later Peter told his readers to verbally share the gospel, here he is giving us a principle for how to witness to those who are the closest to us.

Since these unbelieving husbands would be with their believing wives day in and day out, they would have the opportunity to see if their wives' words about Jesus matched their lives with Jesus. It is most likely that these women came to faith in Jesus some time after their marriages, since the Bible admonishes believers to not be "unequally yoked" with unbelievers (2 Corinthians

6:14). Therefore, these husbands needed to see changed lifestyles, faith with actions, faith lived out. Their wives were to make certain that they walked the talk and were *not* to try to make every single conversation with their husbands about the gospel. In other words, they were to live as godly wives before ungodly husbands.

True lifestyle evangelism means living a Christlike life before unbelievers that includes both godly living and intentionally communicating the good news, whether they take the initiative to ask us about Jesus or not. Our actions and words cannot be separated in true biblical lifestyle evangelism. Though we cannot force people to hear or discuss matters related to Jesus, we do have an obligation to attempt to share his good news with them.

Questions to Consider
- What are your thoughts on the statement that the "message and the messenger are tightly connected?"
- Are there things in your life that hinder you from effectively sharing the gospel? If so, will you look to the Lord for the strength and ability to turn from those things?
- Do you agree that actions are not enough when it comes to lifestyle evangelism? Do you agree that words are not enough when it comes to lifestyle evangelism?

CHAPTER 19

WHAT SHOULD I SHARE IN AN EVANGELISTIC SITUATION?

With the first day of winter quickly approaching, Mark was looking forward to being home for the holidays with family and friends. With this in mind, he wanted to take some time with Roberto this evening to refresh his memory on exactly what to include whenever he explained the gospel.

At Beans, Mark located Roberto and placed his order. "Burr," he murmured as he pulled off his gloves.

"Cold?" Roberto smiled. "Looking forward to Christmas?"

"You know it. Always enjoy this time of the year."

For the next few minutes, they caught up on each other's week and future plans. Then Mark asked if they could begin. "I want to know clearly what to address in an evangelistic encounter."

//

Every encounter is unique because people and situations differ. While I am a fan of learning different models for sharing one's faith with others, I am not a fan of being locked into a single standardized pattern. I view different methods of sharing the gospel like different tools in a carpenter's tool belt. A saw is useful on some occasions, but a hammer is better when driving a nail into a board. You can drive a nail with a saw, but not very well. Good carpenters know how to use their different tools effectively, depending on the situation.

Similarly, many excellent tools exist for evangelism. We need to realize, however, that all methods were developed in specific contexts by specific individuals with certain personalities, gifts, passions, and talents. Listen and learn from their experiences, but don't get locked into a method that doesn't match your personality and the gifts God has given you. The methods you use should allow you to be yourself and to feel confident when you share the gospel with others.

While the message of the gospel does not change, how we communicate it to others varies from situation to situation. I see no evidence of a single method used by Jesus and the apostolic church in the New Testament. For them, the song remained the same, but the instruments used to play that song depended on the audience.

Regardless of the model of personal evangelism, as a rule I encourage sharing at least three things: your personal story, the gospel message, and a challenge. Sometimes you may have a lengthy period of time to share each of these with someone, but at other times you may have only a few minutes.

Your Personal Story

The person you are talking with needs to hear about your life before coming to Jesus, how you came to faith in Jesus, and how Jesus has transformed your life since then. This is the pattern Paul used when speaking to King Agrippa, recorded in Acts 26. While some might deny the gospel message, most people will not reject your personal story. People today want to hear about real experiences, especially those related to the supernatural. For many, truth is somewhat socially constructed, and therefore your personal encounter with Jesus can be an interesting and powerful witness.

The Gospel Message

While our stories are very important, the gospel is the most important story we share. It is the power of God that brings faith for salvation (Romans 1:16–17). This message of the death and resurrection of Jesus speaks to the needs of people today. (For more guidance see chapter 2).

A Challenge

We need to ask our hearers to respond in some manner. While not all situations will allow us to present the entire gospel message and ask for repentance and placing faith in Jesus, we should still close with a challenge. This might come in the form of asking the person we're speaking with to read the Bible, to accept and read a gospel tract, to talk with a pastor, or to check out an evangelistic website.

Questions to Consider

- Have you ever been trained in personal evangelism? If not, consider going through the process, whether formally with a group or class or informally, such as reading a personal evangelism book. (See the "Books to Consider" section in the back of this book.)
- Do you believe a personal story is a powerful witness? Why or why not?
- What are the similarities and differences in how Jesus talked with Nicodemus (John 3), the Samaritan woman (John 4), and the demon-possessed man (Mark 5:1–20)?

CHAPTER 20

WHAT IF I DON'T FEEL LIKE SHARING THE GOSPEL?

"Man, I'm worried about something," Mark said, sipping his espresso.

"What's that?"

"Sometimes I don't have much enthusiasm for sharing my faith. To tell you the truth, sometimes I have no desire to tell others about Jesus. I just don't feel like it," Mark confessed. "What's wrong with me?"

"To borrow a phrase from *The Chronicles of Narnia*, you're a son of Adam."

"A what?" Mark asked, with tension in his voice.

"The book. You know, C. S. Lewis . . . big movie . . ."

"I know about the book. What do you mean, a son of Adam?"

Roberto chuckled, sitting back in his chair. "Just that you are human. We all struggle with our feelings."

"But whenever I hear people talk about sharing their faith, they are always so excited! Their enthusiasm is contagious, and I want that but don't always have it."

"Mark, check out the barista," Roberto said, nodding toward the counter.

"You mean Jazzman Jones?"

"You call him Jazzman?"

"Everyone does. His real name is Dave Jones. He's a big Miles Davis and Stanley Jordan fan. Haven't you noticed that every time he's working, jazz is playing in the shop? Anyway. You were saying . . ."

"Check out Jazzman. Do you think he *feels* like coming to work every day?"

"Dude, no way. He and I talk often, and I know. He's a true 1960s nomadic hippie, living in the body of a twenty-first-century college student, bio/premed major."

"Premed!" Roberto exclaimed. "He's premed? No way!"

"Don't judge a book by its cover," Mark said with a smile.

"Or by its dreadlocks, tattoos, and piercings," Roberto sarcastically retorted. "OK. The point I'm trying to make is that life is not always about feelings. People come to work even when they don't feel like it. We pay our bills when we don't feel like it. The same is true with our faith. We follow Jesus—"

"Even when we don't *feel* like it."

"You got it," Roberto replied. "But let's take a look at some passages that I think will be of some encouragement and help to you."

//

Feelings can be interesting. They can be helpful but also deceptive.

I can echo the concern Mark expressed to Roberto. I *often* don't feel like sharing the gospel with others—and I have a Ph.D. in evangelism and teach evangelism courses! I'm not supposed to feel this way—right? But this matter is simply part of the fact that our flesh is at war with our spirit. What we know we should do, we don't do, and what we know we should not do, we do (Romans 7:15–25). But the good news is that we have grace from our Lord. We should take encouragement from Paul's words: "Wretched man that I am! Who will deliver me from this body of death? Thanks be to God through Jesus Christ our Lord!" (vv. 24–25).

I remember sitting in my vehicle outside a hair-styling shop, praying to the Lord for the strength and desire to walk through an open door from the Lord to share my faith with the woman who would be cutting my hair. I was not in the mood to share the good news. I wish I could say this was a one-time occurrence, but it was not. Many times I have to stop and repent of my lack of desire to do what the Lord wants me to do. And I have found that the Lord deals graciously with his children when the heart's desire is to serve him but the desires of the flesh interfere.

When we make it a regular and intentional practice to share our faith with others, the desire often comes with the practice. The times I have made personal evangelism a regular part of my life are the times when I have found myself feeling more motivated to witness. But when I am not witnessing regularly, I find it more difficult to get motivated to do so. The neglect of the spiritual discipline of sharing our faith extracts the moisture of zeal from the soul, leaving it like a dessert.

In addition, being faithful to the Lord does not always mean we will have good feelings. Jesus was always faithful to the Father but was greatly grieved over going to the cross. He was so grieved that he asked for another option if one were possible (Mark 14:36). And I am sure that Paul was not feeling enthusiastic when it came to his imprisonments, stonings, beatings, shipwrecks, and snake bite for the sake of kingdom advancement.

I had a friend who was always very excited about sharing his faith. "There is nothing like the *feeling* you get whenever you personally introduce someone to Jesus and they say yes," he told me. The Lord would later bless me with many experiences like that; however, sometimes while the angels in heaven rejoiced (Luke 15:10) and my friend danced a happy jig with them, I waited and strained for a feeling that sometimes was there and sometimes not. After beating myself up over this, I decided that I was going to be faithful to the Lord regardless of how I felt at the time.

Zeal for the Lord is important, and there are stories in the Old Testament of the zeal of the Lord coming upon specific individuals. But although many times the Spirit emotionally supercharges us to do the will of the Lord, sometimes there is no emotional rush. Sometimes I don't feel like witnessing because of the bad burrito I ate; sometimes I don't feel like witnessing because I'm moody; sometimes I don't feel like witnessing because of sin. The reality is that we cannot be driven by feelings to do what the Lord desires us to do. Serving him is about faithfulness, not feelings!

Questions to Consider

- Do you ever base your obedience to Jesus on your feelings, or do you serve him regardless of how you feel? Can you give an example?
- Why do you think I find it more difficult to share my faith with others whenever it has been a lengthy period of time since I last shared with someone? Have you ever experienced this in your life?

CHAPTER 21

DO I HAVE TO OFFEND PEOPLE WHEN I SHARE THE GOSPEL?

"That's helpful, Roberto, knowing that I can't always depend on feelings," Mark declared. "I thought you would say that, but I just needed some confirmation. Sometimes the zealous feelings are hard to come by, especially when you experience what I experienced the other day on campus."

"What happened? Get into an argument with someone?" Roberto glanced at the clock behind the counter. He needed to leave in a few minutes.

"Not really an argument, because she did all the talking . . . or should I say yelling? A girl from one of my classes cussed up a storm when I asked her about her thoughts on Jesus. Man, it was like, whoa! I didn't see that one coming."

"What did you say?"

"Well, she was talking about her grandfather, a minister, when I asked her about her faith. Thankfully, I do not encounter people with her attitude often. This was a first for me. But you know, I don't want to offend people. I don't like to argue."

"I don't either," Roberto said.

"So when it comes to sharing my faith, do I have to offend people? I mean remember the guy I told you about that just 'lets his light shine'? Does that ever appeal to me after running into Battling Bertha!"

Roberto waited a moment before he replied. "Mark, I think the immediate answer to your question is no—*you* don't have to offend people when sharing Jesus with them. But I believe a better question is 'Do I have to *be offensive* to others?' Remember, the gospel *is* offensive to some, but *you* will catch more flies with honey than with vinegar."

I think most of us clearly resonate with both Mark and Roberto—we don't want to offend others. Few people like to cause trouble. Most of us are wired in such a way that we do not like to rock the boat. I know I don't like to raise the ire of others. And what better way to tick people off than to talk about religion, especially a faith matter that calls people to repent of their sinful ways!

Yet Roberto's response to Mark raises some excellent points about this concern of offending people. We need to keep two things in mind: First, we must realize that individuals confronted with Jesus don't all respond the same way. Second, allowing the cross of Christ to offend people and *being offensive as we talk to people* about the cross are not the same thing.

Confronted with the Gospel

We must keep in mind that individuals who hear the gospel don't all respond alike. The apostle Paul wrote, "For we are the aroma of Christ to God among those who are being saved and among those who are perishing, to one a fragrance from death to death, to the other a fragrance from life to life" (2 Corinthians 2:15–16). To some we are a scent of delight; to others we are the stench of death. The message of the cross is "a stumbling block" to some and "folly" to others (1 Corinthians 1:23). Paul spoke of the "offense of the cross" (Galatians 5:11). As the Holy Spirit convicts individuals of sin, righteousness, and judgment (John 16:8), they begin to feel guilty before God, many times lashing out their frustration on others. Though they are angry at God, they sometimes shoot the messenger—for example, angry people crucified Jesus, stoned Stephen (Acts 7), and ran Paul out of synagogue after synagogue

We simply have to accept the fact that some people will become offended at the message we bring. Yet we must make certain that we do not react by cowering in fear and ceasing to intentionally share the love of God with others. I believe Satan has tempted many of us, myself included, to give in to the sin of fear—and many times we unfortunately follow Satan's desires. We must repent of such sin and call on the Lord to empower us, remembering that he has given us a spirit "not of fear but of power and love and self-control" (2 Timothy 1:7).

Confronted with Gentleness, Respect, and Love

So the first hard reality is that sometimes people will be offended by the gospel as it uncovers their anger at God. The second is that yes, sometimes they will get upset at *us*. But it is always important to follow the apostle Peter's advice and share with gentleness and respect (1 Peter 3:15), as noted in chapter 18, instead of becoming verbally combative.

Mark noted that his situation with the cussing coed was an exception, not the norm. I can also agree with him on this matter. In all of the years of sharing the gospel with people, I have only had a few times when people became extremely angry, and even then no one threatened me with bodily harm. These words from Proverbs are very true: "A soft answer turns away wrath, but a harsh word stirs up anger" (15:1). When we follow them, we will then find that most people are disarmed by our attitude. I have found this to be the case in my witnessing.

We might have the truth of God, but never allow that knowledge to lead to arrogance, pride, or distain for those outside the kingdom of God. Don't let a conversation become a bitter debate where you seek to prove yourself right rather than point others to Jesus. Instead, seek to remain calm, speak the truth in love, and let people know that you respect them because they are created in the image of God and loved by him.

Such witnessing does not mean that we approach sharing the gospel with a laid-back attitude. Neither does it rule out that we must speak with urgency, poignancy, and with much sobriety. At times you might find yourself talking to the self-righteous—as when Jesus spoke to the religious leaders in Luke 13. During those conversations you might need to become more firm. Yet even during such tense exchanges, don't become mean-spirited but continue to share the truth in love and with respect for the other person.

While writing this chapter at my favorite coffee shop, I was interrupted when a former student engaged me in conversation. A man standing nearby overheard our dialogue about a seminary class, and after the student left, he immediately started talking to me about my job as a seminary professor. After he inquired about my teaching and faith, I asked him about his profession. Shortly into the conversation, I asked him if he had a faith tradition, to which he responded that he was Baha'i. After he had made several references to Jesus and quoted several Bible passages from memory, I inquired, "Could you please tell me what you, being Baha'i, believe about Jesus?" To which he surprisingly responded by putting his hands together and bowing his head toward me, saying, "Oh, thank you for asking me to share with you what I believe."

Though I did not agree with many of the things he told me, by applying Peter's words to my life, the Lord opened up a great opportunity for me to share my personal story about Jesus and the gospel with this man. Though I clearly told him where we disagreed, especially over the exclusive claims of Christ, my attitude was not offensive to him. He did not come to place his faith in Christ during this conversation, but he was able to hear the good news in a manner that communicated gentleness, respect, and love.

Roberto was correct. A better way to understand what Mark was asking is to understand that, though the gospel offends some people, we do not have to be offensive to them ourselves. If the good news has changed our lives and we have it to share, then we should live appropriately.

Questions to Consider

- Can you explain the difference between the gospel being an offense and Christ's followers being offensive?
- When you share the gospel, are you serious, humble, and respectful toward others, or is your demeanor harsh, rude, and abrasive? Can you give an example?
- Have you been passive about sharing the gospel out of fear of offending someone? Can you give an example?

CHAPTER 22

WHAT IF I MAKE A MISTAKE WHEN SHARING THE GOSPEL?

"Let's say that I'm attempting not to be offensive," Mark said. "But I have another concern. Do you ever get scared before you share the gospel?"

The question surprised Roberto; they had discussed this matter before. "You mean, afraid of what someone might think or say?"

"Not really. I mean . . . afraid of yourself."

"Myself?"

"Are you ever afraid of making a mistake when you share the gospel?"

"Ahh. Well, not really afraid of making a mistake. There was a time when I was afraid that I wouldn't know how to respond to people's questions. Why? Are you afraid of doing something wrong?"

"Yeah," Mark confessed. "I'm afraid I'll make a mistake when talking to other people about Jesus."

"What kind of mistake?"

"I don't know. Maybe something like saying the wrong thing."

"Would you ever tell someone that Jesus did *not* die on the cross?"

"No, of course not."

"Would you ever tell someone that Jesus did *not* rise from the dead?"

"No way."

"Do you think you would ever tell someone that he should *not* turn from his sins and follow Jesus?"

"Of course not."

"Then I can't figure out what your mistake might be. The real mistake is refusing to talk with others about Jesus."

Mark's anxiety over making a mistake when sharing the gospel is a real concern for many. Sometimes we're afraid we don't know enough about the Bible. Sometimes we fear not being able to answer the questions leveled at us, or saying or doing something that will cause someone to miss the grace of God and spend eternity in hell.

These fears can lead to missional paralysis—fearing so many potential problems that you don't verbally witness at all. While your fears are real, they might come from insecurity or be rooted in sin. Here are several considerations to help you deal with fears of making a mistake when evangelizing.

The Likelihood for Error Is Low

Recognize that unless you tell someone he doesn't need Jesus or you refrain from telling him the good news, the likelihood of making a critical mistake is not very high. Witnessing is about sharing what you have personally experienced with God. It is telling another person how to have an abundant life now and for eternity.

Remember the First Believers

On this side of the cross, resurrection, and ascension, we have more knowledge about Jesus and salvation than many of the first-century believers, who did not have copies of all the books of the Bible and most of whom would not even have been able to read the Scriptures they had access to. We have been blessed with more than what they had. Look back to their bold witness and how the Spirit greatly worked through their willingness.

Remember God's Love

The Lord loves the unbeliever more than we do, and if we are walking in submission to the Spirit's leadership, he will work through our limitations to bring others into the kingdom. The Lord desires the salvation of the person we are witnessing to more than we desire it. If we are being faithful to tell others what Jesus did and what he can do for them, the Lord will honor our efforts.

Worry Is Sin

When you fear making mistakes in your witnessing, confess worry as sin and repent of it. Paul wrote: "The Lord is at hand; do not be anxious about anything, but in everything by prayer and supplication with thanksgiving let your requests be made known to God. And the peace of God, which surpasses all understanding, will guard your hearts and your minds in Christ Jesus" (Philippians 4:5–7). His peace is sufficient for us.

You Don't Have to Know It All

While the Lord does expect us to grow in our knowledge and understanding of the Scriptures, he knows our limitations. It is OK if someone asks a question and you don't know the answer. Say that you will attempt to find the answer and get back to him. But remember, you are called to share primarily what you have experienced and how others can experience Jesus as well.

Questions to Consider

- How does knowing that God loves the lost person more than you do affect your concerns about making a mistake?
- Will you repent of any worry you have about sharing your faith with others?

CHAPTER 23

WHAT IF SOMEONE ASKS ME A QUESTION I CAN'T ANSWER?

"OK, last question," Mark announced with a glance at his watch. "Dude, you have an incredible knowledge about stuff in the Bible! I mean, I want to be on your team for Bible trivia games."

"Thanks, man."

"Oh, that wasn't a compliment! How come you know so much? I think you are a real . . . what is that good eighties word?—a real nerd!" Mark grinned. "Just kidding!"

Roberto smiled. "I've just spent a lot of time reading the Bible, applying it to my life, and walking with the Lord . . . and not so much time playing video games."

"Hey, there's a Bible video game you can download for a few bucks. You move Bible characters around on . . ."

Roberto groaned. "Great!"

"Seriously."

"I am serious."

"Seriously, your knowledge of the Bible is amazing," Mark said. "It's like you know the answer to everything. You are—you're the Bible Answer Man! I knew it!"

"No, I'm not that good. There are things that I don't know."

"Like did Adam have a navel? Listen, here's my concern," Mark said. "Since I don't have all the Bible knowledge that you do, what do I say when I'm sharing my faith and someone asks me a question I can't answer?"

"That's easy," Roberto said, stone faced. "Just lie." He paused for effect. "Gotcha!"

Just the thought of being asked a question and not knowing the answer causes many individuals great anxiety when it comes to witnessing.

Early in my walk with the Lord, I believed that I had to have an answer to every question. I felt that showing my ignorance would embarrass the Lord, and I believed that others' salvation depended on how convincing I could be about the truth of Jesus.

We *should* study the Scriptures to know the things God has revealed, and we *should* study Christian apologetics to learn how to respond appropriately to the tough questions people ask. There's no excuse for remaining ignorant in our knowledge of the Scriptures and how to better respond to questions, but we must understand that no one knows *everything*.

So what do we do when someone asks us a question that we cannot answer? Simply say, "I don't know." Consider these truths from the Bible regarding the importance of speaking out of knowledge:

- "In everything the prudent acts with knowledge, but a fool flaunts his folly" (Proverbs 13:16).
- "Do you see a man who is hasty in his words? There is more hope for a fool than for him" (Proverbs 29:20).
- "Desire without knowledge is not good, and whoever makes haste with his feet misses his way" (Proverbs 19:2).

Here is a liberating thought about personal evangelism: God does not need you or me to be his bodyguard. He does not need us to be his defense. He is big enough to take care of himself. So when someone challenges you with a question you can't answer, don't freak out. Simply say, "You know, that is a very good question. I don't have an answer for you right now, but I will find out. Let's get back together and talk about it."

When you respond to someone's difficult question in a manner such as this, you communicate four values that are important when witnessing: honesty, humility, sincerity, and relationality.

Honesty

Admitting that you don't know something reveals your honesty. You have the power to speak falsely, to make up something just to seem informed. But by admitting your lack of knowledge, you communicate that you are not a know-it-all and that the question has value.

I once shared the gospel with a man in my kitchen. He had come by my house to activate our security system. While I can't recall exactly how the Lord opened up the opportunity for me to share the good news with him, I do remember his question. After we talked about Jesus, sin, salvation, and God, he said, "J. D., I have a question for you. Why doesn't the Bible talk about life on other planets?"

Now, that is not the typical question I normally get after talking about Jesus! However, I could tell that this man asked in all sincerity and truly wanted to know the answer.

I recall my response to him: "You know, that is a very good question, simply because you are asking it. I don't know why the Bible doesn't talk about life on other planets; I don't have an answer for you. I do know that the Bible says that God created everything, and if there is life on other planets, he created that life as well. Also, while I don't know why the Bible is silent on this topic, I do know what the Bible has to say about life on our planet." Then I was able to return the conversation to Jesus. While it is important to respond to people's legitimate questions, it is also important not to get sidetracked and to return as soon as possible to the gospel.

Humility

When you admit that you don't know the answer to a question, you reveal a humility that is a witness to the power of the gospel. Your humility communicates that you don't *have* to know everything, that you are secure in your faith even though you don't know all the mysteries of the universe or everything about the Bible. You also communicate that followers of Jesus keep learning and have minds open to grow.

A humble response shows that you have no need to revile others who back you into an intellectual corner. Proverbs 15:1 says, "A soft answer turns away wrath, but a harsh word stirs up anger." Your humble acknowledgement that you don't know the answer communicates that Jesus is bigger than the conundrums of life.

Sincerity

Admitting that you don't know the answer to a question but are willing to do some research and find one reveals transparency and respect. Rather than simply dismissing the question as nonsense or foolishness, this communicates you are able to show a sincere and personal interest in the concerns of the person you are speaking with.

Relationality

Offering to find out the answer to a person's question provides an opportunity to set up another time when you can meet again to speak about spiritual issues. Your willingness to work on the other person's behalf and meet again reveals that you are more interested in the person than simply making your point and moving on to someone else.

Questions to Consider

- Are you concerned about not knowing enough of the Bible to be an effective witness? If so, please share your concerns with the Lord, repenting of any fear.
- Are you comfortable admitting that you don't know the answer to a question but will work to find an answer? If not, why not?
- Are you honest, humble, sincere, and relational in your witnessing? What do you need to work on in these four areas?

CHAPTER 24

AM I DISOBEDIENT IF I DON'T SHARE THE GOSPEL WITH STRANGERS?

Christmas and New Year's came and went. Mark enjoyed his winter break. Then the new semester began, and Mark continued to work at the pizza shop in the afternoons and most evenings after classes. He was off on Thursdays, and he and Roberto continued meeting together.

The crowd at Beans was down this week. The snow and cold must have kept everyone home. Mark stamped his boots on the sidewalk to knock off the snow before entering the shop. Roberto was getting his usual cup of coffee from Jazzman.

"Hey, Mark!" Roberto said. Mark draped his coat on the back of a chair at Roberto's table. For the next several minutes, he and Roberto talked about the weather, family, his new classes, and work.

"Man, that Jazzman Jones is one strange barista," Roberto observed.

"How so?"

"Just try talking to him. He's difficult to understand. Might be all those piercings in his lip and tongue."

"Oh, Jazzman is cool," Mark replied.

"Question for you," Roberto said. "I had a pastor when I was in college who told his church that if believers could not go door to door, sharing their faith with complete strangers, then they had sin in their lives. What do you think about that?"

"We all have sin in our lives," Mark said with a smile.

"Yeah! But you know what I mean! He was saying that it was disobedience to the Lord if the members of his church did not do evangelism by going door to door."

"I know, I know. That sounds a bit extreme. I don't recall the Bible telling us all the details of how we are to witness, just to do it. Of course the early church did go from house to house sharing the good news. Hmm . . . I'm not convinced of his statement."

"Me either. Our methods can differ from context to context, but the message of the gospel remains the same."

"So are you saying it is wrong to go door to door?"

"Oh, no. Not at all! It is biblical. I support it. I have done it and will continue to do it in the future. The Lord works through that method."

"Roberto, I think there's another matter here worth discussing. What about sharing the gospel with complete strangers? Let's say it is not about going to a stranger's door, but rather meeting strangers in the normal routine of daily life. Is someone being disobedient for not doing this 'cold-call' type of evangelism?"

"You know, Mark, that is a great question! You really did develop some smarts since last semester!"

"I'm so glad you finally acknowledged my brilliance!"

//

The simple answer to Mark's question is, yes, we are being disobedient if we have determined that we will not share the gospel with strangers we encounter throughout our lives. While I recognize this statement may sound harsh, and definitely not what is commonly advocated in many evangelical circles today, my response is based on the Scriptures.

The expectation found in Scripture is that we will evangelize strangers. As we've seen in previous chapters, we are told to make disciples, be Jesus' witnesses, and preach the word (Matthew 28:19; Acts 1:8; 2 Timothy 4:2). While the specifics are not stated, most examples of evangelism in the Gospels and Acts are with total strangers: Jesus and the Samaritan woman, Jesus and the Gerasene demoniac, Stephen and the religious leaders, Philip and the Ethiopian, Peter and Cornelius, Paul and Silas with Lydia, and Paul and Silas with the Philippian jailer. If we refrain from sharing with those strangers God puts in our paths and only share our faith with those with whom we have established relationships, we fail to follow the predominant model used by Jesus and the apostolic church.

It is important that we are open to the Lord bringing strangers across our paths with whom he would have us share his truth. The following are two principles to guide our daily journeys.

Be Prepared

As followers of Jesus we must be prepared to share the gospel with anyone, at any time, in any place. Paul told Timothy to preach the word in times of convenience and in times when it was not convenient (2 Timothy 4:1–5). We would do well to follow this counsel and always be prepared to give a reason for the hope we have in Christ (1 Peter 3:15). If we share only with those close to us, we will quickly run out of people to witness to and miss out on many wonderful opportunities the Spirit brings our way.

Be Intentional

The missional life consists of joyful and delightful intentionality and regularity when it comes to evangelism. We must always be praying and looking for opportunities to share our faith. Our lives are marked by the purpose of being Christ's ambassadors; God is making his appeal to the world through us as we implore others to be reconciled to God through Christ (2 Corinthians 5:20). I have yet to hear of a national ambassador who is not intentionally and regularly engaged in hard work representing his or her country in foreign lands.

In a New York City cab, on my way to the airport after teaching a class, the cab driver and I started talking. A few minutes into our conversation, he asked if I was married.

"Yes," I replied, "for fourteen years."

Looking up into the rearview mirror, the driver then asked, "Do you still love your wife?"

Now, I have been asked many things in life, but this was one question no stranger had ever asked me. "Oh yes," I said.

"You did not even hesitate to answer my question," the driver said, glancing at me again in his mirror. "That's surprising. When I ask that question to most people, they usually take a moment or two before responding. What is the secret to staying in love with someone for that long?"

Wow! What an opportunity to talk about how Jesus is the reason my wife and I still love each other and how he has transformed our marriage. "Well, since you asked," I replied, "I know this may sound strange, but both my wife and I are followers of Jesus Christ." And so the dialogue continued with a wonderful opportunity to talk about my faith.

Here was a complete stranger. Here was a door of opportunity to share the good news. I had two options before me: I could think, *This guy is a total stranger. He does not trust me. We have no previous relationship. Spiritual matters are too personal to talk about with complete strangers. Therefore, I'll just tell him that my wife and I work hard* [which we do] *at our marriage and make it work,* or I could use the opportunity to point to Jesus and allow the Holy Spirit to work with the gospel message.

Questions to Consider

- Can you recall a time when you talked to a stranger about Christ? Describe it.
- While it might not be your preferred way to evangelize, are you willing to share the gospel with total strangers if the Lord opens those doors? If not, why not?
- If you have concerns about sharing the gospel with strangers, plan to talk to someone about this and seek the Lord for clarity and strength.

CHAPTER 25

WHAT SHOULD I DO IF MY CHURCH IS NOT EVANGELISTIC?

"OK, since your pastor in college had that perspective of evangelism, I take it that your church in college was evangelistic," Mark said.

"Yeah, somewhat."

"I'm thankful that our church is evangelistic," Mark confessed.

"Me too. Unfortunately, most are not. I read a few months ago that most churches in the United States are not reaching their communities with the gospel and seeing people baptized."

Mark took a bite of his dessert. "What is a person to do if he or she is a part of one of those churches?"

"What do you mean?"

"You know, what can people do to help their churches be missional, engaging their communities and the world with the gospel?"

//

Doing the work of an evangelist is simply a part of the life of a follower of Jesus. While the following suggestions could seem to advocate that evangelism is a program to be implemented in a local church, such is not the case. They are to assist you in helping your church as a whole to be obedient to the commands of Jesus. These guidelines are not provided to help you develop a program but to help you influence your church for the sake of the kingdom.

While it is essential that churches be evangelistic, I will address these matters on an individual level. Because unless the individuals making up the church repent and obey Jesus, little will happen on the corporate level. The guidelines that follow should help you create an atmosphere among the believers that evangelism is something everyone does intentionally as you journey through life together.

Pray before Acting

Before doing anything, begin with prayer. Seek the Lord for wisdom to know how to take action regarding your concerns about evangelism. Pray for guidance, humility, and that the Lord's purposes would prevail (Proverbs 19:21). Intercede on behalf of the church and its leaders that necessary changes to advance the kingdom would take place.

Examine Your Walk

Before approaching anyone in the church with your concerns, do some introspection. Jesus warned:

> Judge not, that you be not judged. For with the judgment you pronounce you will be judged, and with the measure you use it will be measured to you. Why do you see the speck that is in your brother's eye, but do not notice the log that is in your own eye? Or how can you say to your brother, 'Let me take the speck out of your eye,' when there is the log in your own eye? You hypocrite, first take the log out of your own eye, and then you will see clearly to take the speck out of your brother's eye" (Matthew 7:1–5).

How is your own involvement in personal evangelism? Are you evangelistic and intentionally sharing your faith with others? If not, make certain you are "practicing what you are preaching" before you start voicing your concerns.

Share Your Heart

Start with the leadership, for they are the key to transitioning a church to being missional. With all humility, begin by sharing with your pastors your concern about the church's commitment to evangelism. Realize that if you have a burden on your heart, the Lord might be planning to use *you* to bring healthy change to the congregation. You might be asked to take responsibility and provide guidance to the church on this matter.

If your leaders are already evangelistic, they need to know that they have your support on leading the church to be focused on making disciples. Your words of encouragement and your way of life will be a blessing to them. If they are not evangelistic, then your voiced concerns will bring this matter to their attention.

Start Small

In our zeal for change and health, we can sometimes overwhelm those who do not yet have the same vision, although there is no excuse for disobedience. If the church currently isn't evangelizing at all, attempting to involve the people in large-scale evangelistic activity is similar to telling a new runner to begin by running a marathon.

We need knowledge and understanding about the church and its members, rather than making haste and missing the way (Proverbs 19:2). Grand plans and programs can be helpful, but often it's best to begin by doing something small and allowing it to grow. Challenge the people to begin praying for the salvation of family members, friends, and the community. Lead a training session, teaching others how to share their faith. Use this book to start a discussion with a small group in the church. Encourage others to share the gospel with someone in the next week.

Recruit Others

Invite others to join your efforts, if permitted. But don't simply make a generic announcement asking others to help you in missional labors in the community; make personal contacts and invitations first. Mass invitations usually do not lead to much commitment, especially invitations related to evangelistic involvement. Instead, approach individuals and ask them to assist you. Help them understand that their examples in personal witnessing will help lead others to such good works for the kingdom.

Trust the Lord

Begin with the people the Lord raises up to assist you in leading the church to be more evangelistic. In all likelihood, you will be blessed with a few rather than many. Do not allow the numbers to discourage you. Work with those committed individuals to reach out to the community. In the future, these few will be able to recruit others to assist in the efforts.

Share Results

Both the pastors and the church as a whole need to know what the Lord is doing through your outreach. Keep the people up to date. Share stories of how individuals in the church are witnessing for Christ. Share mistakes and what is going well. Speak about it in conversations, blogs, e-mails, and if provided the opportunity, share with the church from the pulpit. The stories you tell will encourage, convict, and motivate others to adopt a missional lifestyle.

Questions to Consider

- What are three things you can do to assist your church in the area of evangelism over the next twelve months?
- Why do you think it is important to share stories with the church about what the Lord is doing in the lives of those who are sharing the gospel?

CHAPTER 26

WHAT IF I CAN'T MEMORIZE ALL THOSE BIBLE VERSES?

"Roberto, I have a confession to make," Mark said with a smile. "I am having a difficult time memorizing the first nine chapters of Leviticus so that I can be effective at sharing my faith with others."

"Leviticus? What are you talking about?"

"Scripture memory! Memorizing verses, tons of verses, so I can share my faith. Not Leviticus. I was just kidding about that. But the truth is that while I have memorized some verses, I definitely have not memorized all the verses that you have."

"Well, I've been a believer for a lot longer than you have," Roberto reminded him.

"Yeah, but you know that book I'm reading on evangelism? I get the feeling from the author that I have to memorize a lot of Scripture in order to share my faith effectively."

"I see," Roberto said.

"I mean, I have a hard enough time memorizing material for my exams at school."

"I hear you, Mark. And you know that I'm totally supportive of the discipline of hiding God's Word in our hearts, and I know you are as well. But are you asking if someone must memorize much of the Bible in order to be able to share the truth of Jesus?"

"Well, I know that is not the case, but sometimes I wonder if people use that as an excuse."

//

Some people believe that in order to be effective at evangelism, they must have a lot of Scripture memorized. And that if they don't, they should not be involved in witnessing. A lame excuse? Of course. But it is worth our time to examine it.

Scripture is integral to the lives of believers. We read Scripture to learn about God. The apostle Paul wrote, "All Scripture is breathed out by God and profitable for teaching, for reproof, for correction, and for training in righteousness, that the man of God may be competent, equipped for every good work" (2 Timothy 3:16–17). God works through his Word to save us and to nourish us in truth. We should be in the Scriptures as our daily spiritual food. The better we understand the Scriptures and the more we memorize them (Psalm 119:11), the better we will be at sharing with others the truth we know. There is no substitute for memorizing God's Word.

Who Said You Have to Memorize Leviticus?

While I am going to recommend a few verses to memorize, the truth is that we do not have to memorize large portions of the Bible to share the truth of Jesus. We must remember that we can always tell what we have personally experienced—as Peter and John said, "We cannot but speak of what we have seen and heard" (Acts 4:20). But we should also remember that God's Word is living, active, sharp, and more powerful than anything we can say about it (Hebrews 4:12). So it is important that we are able to share our personal experiences and weave God's Word into our testimonies.

We have already memorized e-mail addresses, phone numbers, Social Security numbers, passwords, and birthdays. So I know we can memorize some Bible verses. I will guarantee that the overwhelming majority of the readers of this book are able to memorize John 3:16. This passage tells the gospel in a nutshell. Memorize it. Share it with others, challenging them to repent and place faith in Jesus.

Carry a Marked New Testament

One excellent way to be prepared to share from the Scriptures is to keep a small New Testament with you (or even an electronic copy), with certain passages marked for ease in referencing them. For example, in the cover of the Bible you could write "Romans 3:23" along with the page number. When you turn to Romans 3:23, underline the passage and write in the margin "Romans 6:23" along with that page number. Underline this passage and write "Romans 5:8" and its page number in the margin. Finally, after underlining Romans 5:8, write "Romans 10:9, 13" in that margin along with its page number. This marked New Testament will provide you with several significant verses of Scripture to use when sharing the good news with others. These verses in Romans are sometimes called the Romans Road to Salvation. I have used these few verses many times in sharing God's love with others. Even if you are not good at memorizing, start small and set a personal goal to memorize these important passages.

Carry a Tract

If you don't wish to use a marked Bible, then you may want to consider getting a good tract with a clear, biblical presentation of the gospel. Many such tracts contain excellent Bible passages. Some can be downloaded to your cell phone. Also there are some good websites you could use if you have access to the internet when you are out in public. If someone will allow you, you can simply sit with them and read through the presentation together, stopping along the way to discuss the different points. One such link that I often use is http://www.sbts.edu/documents/GRACE.pdf.

Questions to Consider

- Have you ever used the excuse that you cannot share your faith because you don't know enough Scripture?
- What are some ways to keep significant verses accessible to you when you are sharing your faith?
- Will you make a plan to memorize the Romans Road to Salvation, if you have not already done so? If not, why not?

CHAPTER 27

WHAT IS THE SINNER'S PRAYER?

"Roberto, one more question—what is the Sinner's Prayer?" Mark asked.

"You know what that is," Roberto replied.

"Well, yeah. I know what it *is*, but what does it do? I used to think that the prayer saved a person, but that can't be true since Jesus does all the saving. And why are there so many versions of it?"

"You're right; the prayer doesn't save anyone. Versions?" Roberto responded, wrinkling his brow.

"I have some gospel tracts at home with a Sinner's Prayer in them," Mark explained. "The prayers are similar but different. I saw an old Billy Graham Crusade on television recently too. After Mr. Graham asked everyone to come forward, he asked them to say a prayer. It also was similar to those in some of my tracts, but not exactly the same."

"Oh, I understand what you are asking," Roberto said. "I've heard several questions here, so let's take them one at a time."

//

The *sinner's prayer* is a fairly recent development in the history of the church. With the rise of evangelicalism, particularly in the United States, the sinner's prayer came to be a tool used in evangelistic work. In all likelihood, the sinner's prayer came into use in the early twentieth century, with Bill Bight (Campus Crusade for Christ) and Billy Graham popularizing it.[1] While we could say that the cries of the ten lepers (Luke 17:13), the tax collector (18:13), and the thief on the cross (23:42) are examples of sinners' prayers (not to mention many others in the Bible), clearly what the contemporary church has come to call the sinner's prayer looks much different.

The sinner's prayer is a declaration from a person's repentant heart to God, confessing that he is a sinner separated from God, that he is repenting of sin, and that he believes in Jesus' death, burial, and resurrection and Jesus' lordship over his life.

Variations of the Prayer

Since the sinner's prayer does not save a person, most variations are to be permitted. I have used various forms of prayer in guiding people to profess faith in Jesus. After sharing the gospel with someone who then wants to follow Jesus, I will ask the person to tell the Lord of this desire.

Now, I know that all that is necessary for an individual to be saved is to believe in the Lord Jesus (Acts 16:31). However, guiding someone to express his desires to the Lord is a matter of pastoral counseling. If he says he would like to speak with the Lord, I invite him to use his own words. If he wants me to lead in a prayer, I always explain a few things: First, that the prayer does not bring salvation. Salvation is by grace alone through faith alone (Ephesians 2:8–9). Second, that the prayer will mention acknowledging being a sinner and turning from sin, that Jesus died for sin and rose from the dead, and that Jesus is Lord. If these statements reflect the person's heart, then he can pray this to God.

While variation exists, a sinner's prayer could go something like this: "Thank you for loving me. I believe Jesus died to pay for my sin and was raised from the dead. I am turning from my sin and placing my faith in you right now. I confess Jesus as Lord. Show me how to live and help me to follow you always. In Jesus' name I pray. Amen."

The sinner's prayer is not some magical incantation, manipulating God like a voodoo charm. Many people have been saved without praying at the moment they first believed in Jesus. How? They did what the Bible says to do: they repented of their sin and placed their faith in Jesus to save them.

Concerns with the Prayer

Unfortunately, there are many people who are so convinced that the sinner's prayer saves a person that they will emphatically declare that if you have not "prayed the prayer," you are not saved. They treat the prayer as if it were a sacrament, and they attempt to relate a person's assurance of salvation to the prayer prayed. Such theology should greatly concern us, for if such is the case, then the only people who have been saved throughout history have been those born after this prayer came into existence.

Such an erroneous belief makes the prayer the key to salvation, much like an animistic incantation. I recall sharing the gospel with a young man and leading him through praying a sinner's prayer. After I returned home, I began to rethink my conversation with him. I found myself worrying that I might have left out some important words in the prayer. This concern weighed heavily on me, for I felt that it was very possible that I had not led the young man to pray as he needed to in order to be saved. My soul found comfort only after I grew in a proper understanding that salvation is by grace alone through faith alone and in the power of the Holy Spirit.

Value in the Prayer

But is there any value in the sinner's prayer? I would say yes, there is. While the sinner's prayer does not save anyone, it does assist them in making a public declaration that marks the moment in time when they volitionally repented of their sin and confessed Jesus as Lord of their lives. Just as the Israelites were commanded to erect pillars of rocks as memorials to the works of the Lord in their lives, the sinner's prayer serves a commemorative purpose. While I believe the Holy Spirit has already worked regeneration in the life of the person before he prays, the prayer erects a spiritual memorial, a marker in time.

Questions to Consider

- Have you placed too much value in the sinner's prayer in the past? If so, how?
- In your own words, explain the value and the abuse of the sinner's prayer?

CHAPTER 28

HOW DO I BEGIN CONVERSATIONS ABOUT SPIRITUAL MATTERS?

Mark had become aware that, although he'd been sharing his faith over the past year, he still struggled with talking to people about spiritual matters. One of his biggest challenges was transitioning a conversation from the ordinary matters of life to the spiritual realm. He hoped to talk with Roberto about this at their meeting tonight.

"I hear you, man," Roberto said. "At times I find that a challenge too. Now, I recognize there is no dichotomy between the natural and the supernatural in a person's life, for we are all spiritual beings. However, it is sometimes difficult to bridge the gap between the mundane and the divine. I think we will always wrestle with this."

"Does it get any easier?" Mark asked.

"Yes, it's kind of like a muscle you have to exercise to improve. The more I share the good news, the more comfortable I feel doing it. When I go through a lengthy period of time when I haven't talked with anyone, I find it to be more of a challenge to bridge the conversation gap with the next person."

"What are some things that help you move from talking about the ordinary things of life to the extraordinary?" Mark asked.

//

We need to overcome the difficulty of transitioning a conversation to the topic of spiritual matters. While I do believe we will find it a challenge at times to talk with some people, the truth of the matter is that people are spiritual beings, and most are willing to share their spiritual experiences and beliefs if we let the Spirit lead us and if we approach people with respect.

When I first started sharing my faith on a regular basis, I was introduced to a book that promoted a high-pressure, psychologically manipulating, sales-oriented method for doing evangelism. I did not know there was another way, so I devoured the book and immediately began applying the methodology to my practice. Several times when I was talking with someone, I could tell that he did not want to discuss any spiritual matters. But believing that the salvation process was dependent on my control of the situation—rather than trusting in the Lord's leading—I found myself trying to force people into a discussion.

I remember being at my university and walking up to a girl who was crossing the campus. I introduced myself and my friend and told her we were out talking to students about spiritual matters, all the while continuing to walk alongside her. It was obvious she had no desire to speak with us because she started walking faster and faster. The more I talked, the faster she walked. And the faster she walked, the faster we walked. Before we decided to let her go on her way, we were literally running side-by-side!

Here is an important truth to Spirit-guided witnessing: If we are intentionally attempting to share the gospel and the person clearly is not willing to talk about such matters, then we do not have to attempt to force open the conversation door. Remember, salvation is of the Lord. He can open doors that we cannot open. We simply need to be willing, available, and intentional in our efforts. Some of the best gospel presentations that I have given have been those that flowed naturally from the conversation at hand.

The rest of this chapter provides additional guidelines to assist you in beginning conversations about spiritual matters.

Pray

Prayer must be an ongoing part of your fellowship with the Father. Prayer is a vital component to seeing a conversation transition from the mundane to the truths of Jesus. Paul wrote, "At the same time, pray also for us, that God may open to us a door for the word, to declare the mystery of Christ, . . . that I may make it clear, which is how I ought to speak" (Colossians 4:3–4). We need to pray before and during our interactions with others, that the Lord would guide our conversations and that he would provide an opportunity for us to share the gospel in a way that allows others to understand and place faith in Jesus.

Look for Opportunities

We need to be watching for what the Lord will do next. If we are willing to look, we will find numerous opportunities to speak about spiritual matters. People will sometimes ask why we think or act the way we do, and that is an opportunity to share how the Lord affects our daily lives. Others might ask some of life's big questions, such as why tragic events happen. People talk about babies being baptized, supernatural experiences, fate, luck, church, hope, peace, fear, religion, and so on. Be listening for points in the conversation that bridge to the good news.

Some people wear crosses on their necklaces; others have tattoos of crosses or other religious symbols on their bodies. These can be conversational bridges too. If unbelievers are bold enough to wear crosses for the world to see, let alone permanently paint them on their arms, they are probably willing to talk about these symbols. So ask about them.

I remember talking about names with a guy in a gourmet popcorn store. He wanted to know what my initials stood for. After telling him my name, he told me his first and middle name and the name that he wished that his parents had named him—Luke. I told him that I liked the name Luke and asked if he knew that there was a book in the Bible called Luke. He responded that he did—another conversational bridge.

Once I was getting a haircut when the stylist asked me if I had heard about a plane crash that had occurred that morning in which every passenger died. I acknowledged that I had caught the story on the news. "When it is time for a person to die, I believe that there is nothing they can do to prevent it," she said, and then told me a story illustrating this point from her Muslim tradition.

Here was an opportunity! I could have simply said, "That's nice. Yeah, God's in control of everything." But realizing this was a divine moment *and that the Lord had opened this door of conversation with her for me to talk with her about ultimate reality*, I asked, "Do you know where you are going when you die?"

Now, had I walked into her shop and opened with this question, she probably would have shut her ears and written me off as a religious nut. Yet here was a situation in which the conversation (super)naturally transitioned into this topic of spiritual matters.

"No, I do not know where I'm going when I die," she replied.

"Well, I'm a follower of Jesus, and I know how you can know for certain that you will go to heaven.[1] Do you mind if I share with you how you can know this information for certain?"

"Oh no, please do!" was her simple reply.

And for the next several minutes, I was able to share the gospel with her, answering her questions and hearing her comments.

She did not respond in a rage. She did not scream, "Infidel!" She did not lop off my ear with her clippers. Natural conversation, simple discussion, nothing forced. The door opened, the conversation bridge was there, and thankfully I was able to cross it.

Be Natural

The best conversations I have had with others about Jesus have come when I did not try to force the conversation in a particular direction. For example, walking down the street with a friend and saying something like, "Wow, look at that tree! God created all trees. He loves you. And sent Jesus to die for the sins of the world. Now what do you think about that?" is not what I would call being natural. While the Lord always works in spite of our rough edges, let's try not to be social weirdos! Guiding points in a conversation is one thing; forcing the conversation is another matter. Be intentional in your communications, but don't oppose the natural direction of the conversation. Otherwise, people will feel that they've been sucker punched with your religion.

Take the Step

Ultimately, we want to take the step of moving the conversation from the mundane to the hope of Jesus, and we want to do this lovingly and humbly and as the Holy Spirit guides us. Again, if people indicate that they are not interested in listening, we can only make ourselves available for future conversations.

Share Your Story

I like to share my story of how I came to faith in Jesus and how he is at work in my life today. People are interested in hearing of our experiences; they may not agree with us, but personal stories are very powerful.

After telling the story about my experience, I will sometimes ask, "Have you ever experienced anything like that?" This question allows others to see that I respect them enough to hear of their experiences. The responses I receive help me understand where individuals are in their spiritual journeys.

A word of caution is necessary: if you ask someone about his experiences, be prepared for what you might hear. After sharing my story with a young woman and asking if she had ever experienced anything similar, she said, "Absolutely! Just last night I had a dream in which the devil was chasing after me!" Now, while I'm just biblical enough to believe that God works through dreams, my story did not include anything about a dream. It didn't have anything in it about the devil either. But somehow this young woman was able to connect with me in dialogue over spiritual matters.

Let People Talk

It is so important that we allow people to share their experiences, even if we do not agree with them. I think the title of Ron Johnson's book communicates a great truth: *How Will They Hear If We Don't Listen?*[2] Listening shows others that we value and respect them as people in the image of God and that we are interested in them and their experiences. Allowing people to share does not mean that we believe they are correct or that their experience honors God; it simply shows respect.

Allow people to ask you questions. We all learn by getting our questions answered. Another word of caution is necessary: be prepared for what you will be asked. Remember the man who asked me if the Bible talked about life on other planets? I could have laughed, but if I had, the conversation would have been over. While some might ask questions in a mocking manner or as a way of avoiding a serious conversation—and need to be ignored—this man's question was legitimate; he was not attempting to evade the gospel.

William Fay[3] asks questions and allows people to share what they believe about Jesus, heaven and hell, and salvation. Then he asks, "If what you said was not true, would you want to know?" He places the ball in the other person's court. If the answer is no, the conversation is over. If the answer is yes, they have invited him to share the gospel.

Another approach that I use when someone tells me about a spiritual experience is to ask, "What do you think God could be trying to tell you through that experience?" I don't think it is always appropriate to ask this question. However, if we believe that the Spirit of God is at work in the world, drawing people to the truth, then we must recognize that God works through natural revelation in the process of bringing people to encounter special revelation (for example, Peter's vision about Cornelius in Acts 10:1–8).

Take for example the woman I mentioned earlier in the chapter who said she had a dream about the devil chasing her. Her story went like this:

> In my nightmare, there was a man who kept killing people, and I continued to run from him. Soon he started coming after me, but I could never see his face. Near the end of my dream, I was able to see his face—it was the devil. He was trying to kill me. It was then that I woke up, because I had rolled off the sofa and landed on the floor. I was terrified and was crying. I called my mother, because she is a religious woman, and told her my dream. She asked, "Honey, what have you done that is so bad that the devil is after you?" I told my mother that I had no idea, because I could not figure out what I had done that was wrong.

It was at this moment that the Lord gave me the right question to ask: "What do you think God could be trying to tell you through that experience?" She responded that she did not know. I said that I thought I knew and asked if I could tell her. Of course, she was open to my words. I simply walked her through the gospel, beginning with the facts that all have sinned (Romans 3:23) and that the devil comes to kill and destroy (John 10:10).

Note what I did not do: First, I did not say that God was definitely speaking to her through her dream. I cannot know this for certain, but I can definitely assume the possibility. Second, I did not put her experience on par with the Scriptures. Third, I looked for a way to use the open door that her experience had created to connect her to the God who holds all dream interpretations (Genesis 40:8). I used her experience to take her to Jesus.

Questions to Consider

- Do you find it difficult to bridge conversations from the ordinary matters of life to the good news? If so, why?
- Do you intentionally look for natural opportunities to transition conversations to the gospel? If not, pray that you will become more sensitive during your conversations with unbelievers.

CHAPTER 29

WHAT IS THE BEST WAY TO WITNESS TO FAMILY MEMBERS OR CLOSE FRIENDS?

"That's helpful, knowing how to better transition a conversation," Mark said.

"You know, I'm still learning," Roberto said. "Those are some things that have helped me in the past."

"Hey, who is the most challenging person to witness to?"

"You mean like an agnostic, a Muslim, or an atheist?"

"Just in general," Mark said, not knowing exactly how to ask his question.

Roberto sighed. "Well, personally I have found my family members and close friends to be the most challenging."

"Why?"

"Maybe because they are familiar with me as a person? Maybe because I'm too familiar with them? Or is it because to talk about such matters might strain the relationship? Good question, Mark. I think there are probably many factors involved."

"Interesting. You know, I have heard just the opposite from other people," Mark commented. "I've had a few people tell me that they find it easier to talk with family and friends about the gospel than with strangers."

"Yeah. Every relationship is different. I was just saying what I've experienced."

"What wisdom can you give me that might be helpful when it comes to witnessing to family members and close friends?" Mark asked.

//

Several biblical passages help provide some guidance for Mark's question. Sometimes witnessing to those who are the closest to us is the most challenging. Like Roberto, this is what I have experienced when trying to witness to several family members who are not followers of Jesus. I love them dearly and pray for them regularly, but the challenge is nonetheless present.

Immediate Family and Friends

One passage to consider is found in the first chapter of John's Gospel. Jesus began his ministry by calling the twelve disciples (vv. 35–51). Among the first few called was Andrew, Simon Peter's brother. After coming to Jesus, Andrew found Simon Peter and invited him to meet Jesus. On the following day, Jesus called Philip, and then Philip found Nathanael and told him about Jesus. Much like Nathanael did, family members and friends sometimes will question our beliefs, but our humble response, like Philip's, should be to invite them to investigate Jesus for themselves if they have reservations.

Remember that often it is the closest relationships that allow the strongest witness. Another example of this can be found in John 4. Here the Samaritans came to believe in Jesus because of the testimony of one woman from the village (v. 39). And after Jesus called Levi (Matthew) to follow him, Levi threw a party at his house and invited many of his friends and fellow tax collectors to meet the guest of honor (Luke 5:27–32).

Spouses

A helpful passage related to witnessing to our husbands or wives is 1 Peter 3:1–2: "Likewise, wives, be subject to your own husbands, so that even if some do not obey the word, they may be won without a word by the conduct of their wives, when they see your respectful and pure conduct." As discussed earlier (see chapter 18), however, Peter's teaching here is not that that women should say nothing but simply live a good life before their husbands. As always, the context must be taken into account. Later in the chapter Peter addresses both men and women, saying, "But in your hearts honor Christ the Lord as holy, always being prepared to make a defense to anyone who asks you for a reason for the hope that is in you; yet do it with gentleness and respect, having a good conscience, so that, when you are slandered, those who revile your good behavior in Christ may be put to shame" (vv. 15–16).

As noted previously (see chapter 18), unbelieving husbands would be with their believing wives day in and day out, so they would have opportunity to see if their wives' words about Jesus matched their lives with Jesus. Therefore, these husbands needed to see changed lifestyles, faith in action, faith lived out. Their wives were to make certain that they walked the talk and were *not* to try to make every single conversation with their husbands about the gospel. In other words, they were to live as godly wives before ungodly husbands, letting the power of the gospel show forth.

According to Peter, then, it is one thing for us to tell our spouses that we are followers of Jesus; it is another to prove it every day. I believe that Peter's words are very applicable to all of us with family and friends who are closely watching our lives, knowing that we follow Christ.

Questions to Consider

- Are there family members or friends you need to be more intentional about praying for and more intentional in witnessing to them?
- Are there lifestyle changes you need to make so that family or friends will see how Jesus has changed your life? Is there anything you need to confess to family or friends as acknowledgement that you have been a poor witness for Jesus with your lifestyle in the past?

CHAPTER 30

AFTER I HAVE SHARED THE GOSPEL, MUST I BRING IT UP IN ALL FUTURE CONVERSATIONS?

"Hey, I want to talk about my uncle Ted for a moment," Mark directed.

"You've been witnessing to him for some time," Roberto said.

"Actually, I want to talk about one of his friends, Charlie."

"OK, what about Charlie?"

"Well, part of the reason my uncle is turned off to the faith is that every time Charlie is around my uncle, he *always* is sharing the gospel. I mean, I'm a believer and really want my uncle to come to know the Lord, but I have to admit—and I feel guilty even saying this—Charlie's approach makes me even feel uncomfortable. I also heard my uncle talking to my aunt about wanting to separate himself more from Charlie because he is 'always pushing religion.'"

"Why are you uncomfortable? Is he sharing false information?" Roberto asked, even though he knew what Mark meant.

"No. He is not preaching a false gospel, thank God. He is simply preaching with bad timing. He tries to turn every conversation to spiritual matters and challenges my uncle to repent even when the conversation is miles away from such issues. The dude's heart is in the right place. But he can be walking through a park with my uncle talking about sports and then see a rock, say that Jesus promised to build his church on the rock, and start in with a monologue about Jesus all in a matter of seconds. My uncle can't get a word in edgewise."

"Have you talked with Charlie about it?"

"Once. But I don't know Charlie that well. He's my uncle's friend. I told him my concern and encouraged him to keep praying and witnessing to my uncle. He basically told me that he is to preach the gospel in season and out of season—when it is convenient and not convenient—and that the gospel is the power of God for salvation so he has to get the message into my uncle's ears for it to work. I mean, it is like the dude sees the gospel as some Harry Potter incantation or potion—like if he can get all the right words poured into a person, no matter how crass and rude he has to be, it will work."

"I see." Roberto sighed, knowing what Mark was thinking and feeling, for he had been in several similar situations before—not as the Mark but as the Charlie.

"When I share the good news with someone, how often do I need to return to the topic after we have discussed it? I want to be faithful in my witnessing, but I don't want to become another Charlie," Mark said.

"Let's talk about that. I hear your heart, and I think I know where Charlie is coming from."

//

It is true that we are to preach the message in season and out of season and that the gospel is the power of God for salvation; it is true that people will not come to faith unless they receive the message of hope (2 Timothy 4:2; Romans 1:16; 10:14). But do these truths mean that we must be weird when it comes to witnessing?

Do we have to become inept at carrying on conversations with others unless those conversations include discussions of their need to repent and place faith in Christ? Do we have to become socially uncouth toward unbelievers, unable to function and communicate with them in ordinary ways? Must we share the plan of salvation with others in every future encounter we have with them until we know they are believers?

Ready to Share

Even after we have shared the gospel with someone, we should always be prepared to talk with them again in the future. New questions may arise in their mind; new doors might open—so be ready. Keep praying and looking for those opportunities as the Lord arranges them.

Future Conversations

While we should be ready to share the good news on future occasions, we must realize that humans are social beings. Life cannot function normally if the only spoken message between two people is the same message over and over again. After we have explained the gospel to someone, we should be encouraging conversations about topics other than repentance and faith in Jesus in order to build the relationship.

To many the gospel is offensive and a stumbling block (Romans 9:33; 1 Peter 2:8), but *we* do not have to be. While you and I know the gospel is the most important information anyone can hear, the unbelievers we are speaking to do not know this. In all likelihood they will not appreciate us acting as if we were a scratched record, playing the same message over and over again. Our good intentions will be perceived as insensitive and uncaring, since our actions will be revealing that we do not care about what is on their hearts. Remember, others who know we are followers of Jesus watch our lives to see if they want any part of our way of life.

Old Testament Examples

Throughout the Old Testament we see examples of individuals who lived as witnesses for the Lord among unbelievers. The lives of Joseph, Daniel, Shadrach, Meshach, and Abednego, for example, provide insights for how we should live. They continued to contribute effectively to their society and lived and spoke words of witness whenever the opportunities arose. They were people who showed they could function normally in a community while letting their lights shine.

Wise Words

The book of Proverbs has much to say about words spoken at the right time. We must realize that in our conversations with others, we need to use wisdom and discernment:

- "There is one whose rash words are like sword thrusts, but the tongue of the wise brings healing" (Proverbs 12:18).
- "Do you see a man who is hasty in his words? There is more hope for a fool than for him" (Proverbs 29:20).

- "A word fitly spoken is like apples of gold in a setting of silver" (Proverbs 25:11).

Wise Actions

Prior to sending out the Twelve, Jesus instructed them to be "wise as serpents and innocent as doves" (Matthew 10:16) as they shared the gospel with others. Especially after having witnessed to an acquaintance, we need to pay particular attention to our behavior:

> You are the salt of the earth, but if salt has lost its taste, how shall its saltiness be restored? It is no longer good for anything except to be thrown out and trampled under people's feet.
>
> You are the light of the world. A city set on a hill cannot be hidden. Nor do people light a lamp and put it under a basket, but on a stand, and it gives light to all in the house. In the same way, let your light shine before others, so that they may see your good works and give glory to your Father who is in heaven (Matthew 5:13–16).

Paul also encouraged the use of wisdom when it came to sharing the gospel. Writing to the Colossians, he noted, "Walk in wisdom toward outsiders, making the best use of the time. Let your speech always be gracious, seasoned with salt, so that you may know how you ought to answer each person" (Colossians 4:5–6).

And remember Peter's words (1 Peter 3:1–4) to the wives married to unbelieving husbands, discussed in chapters 18 and 29. The principle found there is applicable here. A gentle spirit, compassion, pure conduct, a respectful attitude, and a consistent lifestyle provide a powerful witness to those who have heard from us the gospel message.

Questions to Consider

- Think of someone you have witnessed to. How can you be an ongoing, wise witness for Jesus to this person?
- What do you think about the statement, "The gospel is offensive, but we don't have to be"?

CHAPTER 31

WHAT DO I DO WHEN SOMEONE SAYS HE WANTS TO FOLLOW JESUS?

As the semester wore on, Mark began looking forward to spring break. This year he and a friend were going camping and canoeing for four days. "No pie or espresso tonight," he told Roberto. "Just a regular cup of coffee. I've got to save some cash for spring break."

"What? No dessert? No espresso?" Roberto asked with an exaggerated expression. "I think I'm going into shock! Are you feeling OK?"

"Shut up! Just black coffee for the next few weeks."

"Just kidding. Well, good for you! I'm proud of you, Mark."

"Well, what are we talking about tonight?" Mark asked.

"I don't know. Hold on a minute. I want to get a piece of pie and a skinny mocha latte with extra foam!" Roberto said.

Mark just glared at Roberto.

Then Roberto added, "Hey, let's talk about the Jazzman's tattoos. I noticed that he has a really cool one that says 'Mom.'"

"It's just Jazzman, not *the* Jazzman! Stop giving him a hard time. He's really a nice guy," Mark replied. "Besides, I happen to know that he loves his mother. Now that you are in a silly mood, what are we talking about tonight?"

After a few more moments of friendly snide remarks from both men, they composed themselves and started talking about the concern of the evening.

"Have you ever introduced people to Jesus who said yes, they wanted to follow him?" Mark asked sincerely.

"Yes. I have."

"Can we talk about what to tell people when they do respond positively to the challenge to follow Jesus?"

"Of course," Roberto said.

//

When someone tells you that he wants to become a follower of Jesus, it is a wonderful thing! But I believe that many of us think, unfortunately, that introducing a person to Jesus is like rocket science. Or we are prone to believe that only professional clergy are capable of taking things to the next level—that we've done the sowing but are not capable of answering the Philippian jailer's question, "What must I do to be saved?"

When I was in high school, I had a friend who was not a follower of Jesus, and I had been sharing the gospel with her for a while. Finally, the day arrived when she said, "Yes, I want to follow Jesus. What do I need to do?"

I froze. I truly did not know what to say. My response? I loaded her into my pickup and drove to meet with one of the pastors of my church.

Why did I not know what to say? Why did I have to locate one of my pastors to guide my friend on this part of her spiritual journey? It was simply because I thought the process of guiding someone across the line from unbelief to belief was a complex task. Now I know that nothing could be farther from the truth.

So have an answer ready when someone says, "Yes, I want to be a follower of Jesus. What do I need to do?" Use the guidelines that follow to help you prepare.

Don't Panic

The first thing to keep in mind is that you do not need to freeze in fear. There is nothing you can or will ever do that will keep someone from the sovereign grace of God. No one's salvation depends on you "winning" them.

Ask a Few Questions

Ask questions to make certain the person you are speaking with understands the gospel message. I first ask people if they understand that they are separated from God and if they know why they are separated from him. I ask them to tell me who is Jesus and why he came into the world, and whether they believe that he is the only Savior and died for their sins and arose from the dead. Last, I ask if they believe if Jesus is Lord. (Because I have unpacked the meaning behind each of these concepts in other chapters throughout this book, I will not reiterate them here.)

Share Simply What the Bible Says

Next, share what the Bible says to do. And what does the Bible have to say regarding this matter? When Paul and Silas were confronted by the Philippian jailer's question, notice what they said: "Then he brought them out and said, 'Sirs, what must I do to be saved?' And they said, 'Believe in the Lord Jesus, and you will be saved, you and your household.' And they spoke the word of the Lord to him and to all who were in his house" (Acts 16:30–32). We can also look at what Paul wrote in Romans, "If you confess with your mouth that Jesus is Lord and believe in your heart that God raised him from the dead, you will be saved. . . . For 'everyone who calls on the name of the Lord will be saved'" (Romans 10:9, 13).[1]

We are to tell people to *believe* in Jesus. Clearly, belief is not simply an intellectual acknowledgement of Jesus and what he did. We must remember that even the demons believe in Jesus and are not saved (Mark 2:24; 5:7). When the Scriptures call people to believe in Jesus, the call is for repentance—a turning away from sin and a turning to God for forgiveness and salvation. The call is for people to agree that Jesus is Lord over the universe and that he died for sin and was raised from the dead on their behalf.

While I am not opposed to leading a person through a prayer of confession (or the sinner's prayer—see chapter 27), we must be biblically honest and admit there is no such act required in the Bible for someone to be saved. No one is told to pray a prayer for salvation, speak to a pastor, be baptized,[2] go through a catechism class, walk an aisle, have an emotional experience, hear the audible voice of God, roll around on the floor, or anything else. And while confession to God is a common and acceptable response, the Bible does not command that someone has to say anything to God to be saved. Those who sincerely believe that Jesus is Lord of their lives are those who are saved and in God's kingdom.

So what are we to tell someone after they have a clear understanding of sin and God's plan of salvation? Simply, "Believe in Jesus. Turn from sin and declare him as Lord of your life." We should encourage them to make this declaration without delay, because "now is the day of salvation" (2 Corinthians 6:2).

Follow Up

The Bible commands us to make disciples (Matthew 28:19), not converts. After confession of Jesus as Lord, the journey begins. Encourage new believers to tell someone else about this good news within the next twenty-four hours.

Within a short time, new believers need to be baptized and to begin to minister with their gifts and talents through a local church that values Scripture. They need to be taught how to pray and how to study the Scriptures. They need to understand the realities of spiritual warfare and how to live the victorious Christian life here and now.

While the scope of this book will not permit me to address the important elements involved in "teaching them to observe all" that Jesus commanded (Matthew 28:20), recognize that it is extremely important for you to follow up with people after their conversions to ensure that they are set on healthy paths. They need someone to mentor them, especially during the early days of their new lives in Christ, much like Roberto mentored Mark. Consider mentoring them yourself or finding others to assist in this process.

Questions to Consider

- If the next person you evangelize tells you they want to follow Jesus, how will you respond?
- Will you commit to teach and mentor someone you see come to faith in Jesus?
- Are you surprised that repentance toward God and faith in Jesus (Acts 20:21) are all that are necessary for someone to enter into the kingdom? If so, why are you surprised?

CHAPTER 32

WHAT DO I DO WHEN SOMEONE SAYS HE DOESN'T WANT TO FOLLOW JESUS?

"Wow, I thought I would get caught in the game traffic tonight. I'm sure glad you got here early and found this table," Mark said. The number of people already in the shop after the game had forced Roberto to stake out a couple of seats near the front door. Mark saw a tall, skinny man with the look of a homeless person come up behind Roberto.

"Excuse me, sir," the man said. "Could you spare some change so I can get a cup of coffee?"

Roberto turned around and smiled. "Well, I think I can do better than that. How about I buy you a cup of coffee?"

"Uh, OK." The man looked surprised.

Roberto introduced himself and Mark. He asked the man's name—John, walked with him to the counter, and invited him to sit with them while he drank his coffee.

After a few minutes of conversation about the university's team, Roberto told John why he and Mark were meeting at Beans. "John, we are both fol- lowers of Jesus. We get together every week to talk about life and what the Bible has to say about how we should live."

"That's good. I go to church sometimes," John said. "Religion is helpful."

"That's great, John, that you meet with a church," Roberto said. "That is important. But one thing we have learned from the Bible is that being a follower of Jesus is about a real relationship with him and not about being religious." Roberto paused to sip his coffee and allow John to take in what he was saying. "You see, religion is about me doing something to attempt to earn God's favor or doing enough good deeds to outweigh my bad deeds so that God will forgive me and let me into heaven."

John nodded.

"But what Jesus offers—what the Bible teaches—is a relationship with God. Jesus did everything on the cross necessary for us to have forgiveness of our sins and to know God personally."

For the next forty-five minutes, Roberto, Mark, and John continued in conversation about the gospel and how it applies to all of life. John had many questions about the Bible, God, Jesus, church, other religions, alcoholism, the Beatles, terrorism, the U.S. government, Vietnam, and taxes. While some of the questions were of consequence, others were not, but Roberto and Mark responded with sincerity to them all.

By the end of the conversation, John had told them that he was not ready to become a follower of Jesus. "But you've given me important things to think about," he said. He thanked them for the time and coffee, shook their hands, and walked out the door and down the sidewalk into the night.

//

When an individual makes it clear to us that he does not wish to follow Jesus, our only response can be to allow that person to continue in his state of bondage and separation from God. We cannot save anyone. We must not manipulate anyone into making a false confession that Jesus is Lord. When we have been faithful at doing our part in sharing the gospel, we must leave the rest of the work in the hands of the Holy Spirit.

In this chapter I'll list some of the practices I advocate for those times when people tell us they are not interested in following Jesus.

Recognize That We're Not the Ones Being Rejected

When people do not respond positively to the gospel, they are rejecting Jesus, not us. We can't take it personally. If our egos are more important to us than Jesus, we need to repent of this pride.

Respect the Decision

While I do not take delight in anyone's decision to reject God's offer of salvation, I must respect his choice. If the church across the centuries had followed this practice, we would not have records of forced "conversions" and Christianization by the sword.

Keep the Door Open

I do not assume that just because someone rejected Jesus today that he will reject Jesus tomorrow. There is both biblical and historical evidence of individuals and people groups who were resistant to the initial presentation of the gospel but later received the good news with gladness of heart. Let those you speak with know that you are always open to continuing the discussion and welcoming of their questions.

Give a Reminder of the Consequences

James wrote that our lives are like a vapor—here today and gone later today (James 4:14 KJV). While it is not always a pleasant matter to remind people of their mortality, I do encourage them to make their decision quickly because none of us is guaranteed that tomorrow will come. This must be done with grace, concern, and love in our voices and without any attitude of arrogance or anger.

Leave a Tract Behind

I know that some of you are thinking, *Tracts? Not cool!* You might be imagining men with greasy, parted hair, in out-of-style polyester suits and ties, giving away these little gospel booklets like candy on street corners.

Tracts are tools. That's all. And they are best used in the context of a relationship or where you have already had the opportunity to dialogue with someone about the gospel. After sharing with people who then tell me that they do not want to follow Jesus, I usually say, "I would like to give you this little booklet that basically summarizes what we have been talking about." I hand it to them and encourage them to read it later and consider our discussion.

The value of a piece of gospel literature is that it can stay with someone after you have left. The Holy Spirit works through such a resource. A person can read it in the privacy of home and consider the claims of Jesus there.

I always try to have such a resource with me wherever I go. In some cases, I have been in a good conversation with someone, only to be interrupted. I have been very thankful to leave such a resource behind in such situations.

Now a disclaimer is in order! I don't use just *any* tracts. I would say that if you use them, be certain they have biblical passages to communicate a clear gospel message, addressing sin, God, our separation from God, Jesus and his death and resurrection, repentance and faith, and some of the immediate steps a person should take after a decision to trust Jesus. I would also encourage you to use resources that are visually appealing.[1] I have seen tracts printed on a church's old mimeograph machine that looked like something a five-year-old designed. If you are sharing the gift of God's love, take care that the package looks good! I would also add that there needs to be a place on the resource where you can provide your contact information for follow up.

Continue to Pray

Make sure you remember in prayer each person who rejects Jesus' salvation offer. Pray for the Spirit to work through your witness and the materials you leave behind. Pray for others to be able to share the gospel with these people as well.

Continue to Look for Opportunities

If you are permitted to have future interactions with someone who has rejected Jesus' offer of salvation, pray and look for future opportunities to share. Don't feel that every future conversation has to address spiritual matters—but be open to these possibilities. People you have witnessed to know the truth you believe, and they now are going to be watching your actions, attitudes, and words. They also will be watching how you treat them in the future, especially because they have rejected *your* Jesus. Be intentional in praying and looking for opportune moments to share the good news again as the Spirit leads you.

Questions to Consider
- Reflect for a moment on Roberto's and Mark's encounter with John. If you found yourself in a similar situation, would you look

for an opportunity to share the gospel? Or would you simply provide John with a cup of coffee or some money, or would you ignore him? Give reasons for your answer.

- Whenever people say no to the gift of Christ, do you feel that they have rejected you? If so, why do you feel this way?

- When someone rejects Jesus, do you have a difficult time respecting his decision? If so, why? What are some practical things you can do to make certain to keep the door open for future opportunities with this person?

- How do you feel about using tracts in witnessing? Would you consider carrying one or two with you? If not, will you consider having something else with you to pass along to others as the opportunities arise (for example, a card with a link to an evangelistic website)?

CHAPTER 33

WHAT IF MY BEHAVIOR WASN'T CHRISTLIKE WHEN I SHARED THE GOSPEL?

"You know, that was the first time I ever watched you talk with someone about Jesus," Mark said.

"You helped too. And you did a great job! I'm proud of you."

"I bet you always do a great job talking with people," Mark said.

"Well, I am humbled by your words of encouragement, but I would not say that," Roberto replied. "I'm just thankful that you did not see me early in my walk with Jesus."

"What do you mean?"

Roberto laughed. "Dude, I was not nice. I was like the Soup Nazi on *Seinfeld*. You no follow Jesus!? No soup for you!"

Mark laughed. "I would have loved to see that! Well, if we are showing all our cards tonight, I have to confess that I've probably been a real jerk with some people as well. You know, now that I think about it, I still see a couple of those people on campus. I wish I could take back the way I treated them."

"What about attempting to make things right?" Roberto asked gently.

"How?"

//

I clearly recall the first time I made an intentional effort to share the gospel with someone. I was in high school and had been praying for my band director for some time. He invited the seniors to go on a day trip during the

Christmas break to see *The Nutcracker* ballet. Since only a few students went, we all had a significant amount of time with him throughout the day. The drive was a six-hour round trip from our town, and I was able to ride up front—which was intentional on my part.

Throughout the day I continued to pray for an opportunity, and on the return trip the Lord opened such a door. As we traveled the interstate toward home, we approached an overpass. "J. D., as we go under this overpass, look at what is written on the inner wall," he said. I looked but saw nothing. Slightly perturbed, having not seen anything himself, my teacher excused the matter, saying, "Oh, well, I guess it is not there."

"What's not there?" I asked.

He chuckled. "Someone put graffiti on the wall that said, 'Jim Morrison is God.'"

Jim Morrison had been the lead singer for The Doors, and my teacher was a great fan of the group, so I wasn't surprised at his excitement over someone's tribute to the deceased. But I immediately recognized that here was the opportunity I'd been waiting for.

"What do you think about it saying Morrison is God? What do you think about God?" I asked.

For the next fifteen minutes, my teacher passionately proclaimed why the Bible is wrong and that Moses had given the children of Israel the Ten Commandments simply to keep order among two million people wandering in the desert. Whenever I attempted to share what I believed, he quickly interrupted and spewed out more of his opposition to the gospel.

I tell this story to say that I wish it had ended on a positive note. Now, you might be thinking that a positive note would be my teacher coming to faith in Christ. *Of course*, that would have been a positive note on which to end. However, a positive note for me at this time also would have been for us to be able to continue our relationship and our dialogue at a future time. But in my attempt to share Jesus with him, I failed to show him love. The more he interrupted me and the more he opposed the truth, the angrier I became. I was so angry that I was biting the inside of my cheek. For the rest of the three-hour drive, I clammed up and never said another word to him. In fact, for the rest of my high school career, I said very little to the man.

I do think that believers should be upset at wickedness. But we need to act appropriately whenever we get upset at the right things. This man acted and spoke as he did because he was lost, and I acted inappropriately in response. We cannot expect unbelievers to act, talk, and think like believers. A missional lifestyle is one that stands up for the truth but does not berate the darkness. If we are going to live for Jesus, we are going to have to put up with a great deal of garbage that comes from the trash heap of the kingdom of darkness. Evangelism is dirty work.

When we find ourselves in situations like mine, is all lost? No. Are our relationships forever severed? Maybe, but probably not. So what are we to do?

Repent

First, if the Lord has revealed to you that you sinned in such a manner, even when attempting to share the gospel, just repent. It's that simple. Jesus still loves you. He died for you. And his grace is sufficient for you. If he can use the rotten scoundrels found throughout the Bible from Genesis through Revelation, he can still use a humble sinner like you to advance the kingdom for his glory.

Remember, God desires that people be saved even more than you do. Your mistake will not keep a person out of heaven. Just repent and be restored to fellowship with the Lord and move on. Don't wallow in your mistake.

Confess

If possible, return to the person you offended and apologize. Confess your sin to him, letting him know that your actions and words were not Christlike and that the Lord wants you to attempt to make amends with him. Here is an opportunity for another powerful witness for the gospel: Let him know that believers are not perfect and that you messed up and are sorry.

Attempt to Restore the Relationship

Ask for forgiveness and an attempt to start over. Such transparency, honesty, humility, and brokenness are a powerful testimony to the gospel. If the person accepts your apology, the relationship continues. Or he might continue to spout blasphemy and tell you that your apology reveals that all believers are weak and too concerned about what others think, and that he wants nothing to do with a weak Jesus. Regardless, you will have made an attempt to reconcile the relationship, and God will use your attempt for his purposes.

Questions to Consider

- Have you ever acted inappropriately when you attempted to share your faith? Why did you act the way you did? Is there something you should do now because of how you acted in the past?
- What are some things that have upset you when you've attempted to talk with unbelievers about Jesus? Is there something you can do now to better prepare yourself for future situations that could involve these frustrations?

EPILOGUE

Near the end of the semester, Mark was delighted to be with one of his friends when he came to faith in Jesus. Roberto encouraged Mark to begin following up with his friend immediately, teaching him spiritual disciplines such as Bible study, prayer, fasting, fellowshipping in a local church, using his spiritual gifts, and witnessing.

Mark soon faced a dilemma. Because of his schedule with school, work, and church, he could not meet weekly with both Roberto and his friend. Fearing that Roberto would be disheartened, he prepared himself for breaking the news to his mentor. But Roberto was thrilled that Mark was willing to end their time together in order to pour his life into this new believer. He told Mark that he had made the right decision and sent him away with his blessing. By the beginning of the summer, Mark was mentoring his friend in the faith.

One Sunday as Mark was talking to Roberto just before their worship gathering, Roberto announced that he was about to start mentoring again.

"Who is it?" Mark inquired.

"I don't know for sure," Roberto replied. "One of the guys who was baptized recently. I'm waiting to meet him this morning. Dave something. Dave Jones, I think."

"Jazzman Jones!" Mark shouted with laughter. "You and the barista from Beans! That's great!"

It was at that moment Roberto heard a deep, sluggish voice behind him. "Whattzz up? Hey man, are you Roberto? Pastor told me some Hispanic guy is my new mentor and to meet him here. Are you him? I'm Jazzman."

With eyes wide as saucers and an empty feeling in his stomach, Roberto slowly turned around to gaze at the infamous barista—tattoos, piercings, dreadlocks, and all. "Man, I now love Jesus," Jazzman said. "And I love you too, bro! When are we meeting this week?"

"Just remember," Mark whispered. "He's premed and he loves his mom!"

NOTES

Chapter 2
1. Ronald F. Youngblood, ed., *Nelson's New Illustrated Bible Dictionary* (Nashville, TN: Thomas Nelson, 1995), 516.
2. Mark McCloskey, *Tell It Often, Tell It Well: Making the Most of Witnessing Opportunities* (San Bernardino, CA: Here's Life Publishers, 1986), 21–26.

Chapter 3
1. Psalm 119:11.
2. Acts 17:11.
3. For more verses related to repentance, see the following: God told Israel to repent and turn from their idols (Ezekiel 14:6). Repentance brings life (Ezekiel 18:32). John the Baptist called people to repentance (Matthew 3:2). Jesus called people to repentance (Mark 1:15; Luke 5:32). The apostles preached repentance (Mark 6:12, Acts 2:38; 3:19; 8:22). Repentance is necessary for salvation (Luke 13:3). Paul called people to repent (Acts 17:30; 20:21). God's kindness to people leads them to repentance (Romans 2:4). The Lord uses sorrow to bring about repentance (2 Corinthians 7:9). God grants people repentance (2 Timothy 2:25). The Lord does not wish for any to perish, but for all to come to repentance (2 Peter 3:9).
4. Wayne Grudem, *Systematic Theology: An Introduction to Biblical Doctrine* (Grand Rapids, MI: Zondervan, 1994), 713.
5. Thomas Watson, *The Doctrine of Repentance* (Carlisle, PA: The Banner of Truth Trust, 1987), 18.

Chapter 4
1. Ephesians 1:5.

Chapter 5

1. Additional passages on conversion include the following: Deuteronomy 4:30; 1 Samuel 7:3; 1 Kings 8:33; Isaiah 19:22; 55:7; Jeremiah 3:12-14; 25:5; 35:15; Ezekiel 18:21–23; 33:11; Joel 2:12; Amos 4:6–8; Hosea 7:10; Malachi 3:7; Matthew 13:15; 18:3; Luke 1:16; John 12:40; Acts 3:19; 9:35; 14:15; 15:19; James 5:19-20.

Chapter 7

1. J. I. Packer, "Regeneration," in *Evangelical Dictionary of Theology*, 2nd ed., Walter A. Elwell, ed. (Grand Rapids, MI: Baker Academic, 2001), 924.

Chapter 10

1. Lewis A. Drummond, *The Word of the Cross: A Contemporary Theology of Evangelism* (Nashville, TN: Broadman Press, 2000), 278.

2. Additional passages on election include the following:

"Blessed is the nation whose God is the LORD, the people whom he has chosen as his heritage!" (Psalm 33:12).

"You whom I took from the ends of the earth, and called from its farthest corners, saying to you, 'You are my servant, I have chosen you and not cast you off'" (Isaiah 41:9).

"Before I formed you in the womb I knew you, and before you were born I consecrated you; I appointed you a prophet to the nations" (Jeremiah 1:5).

"I have loved you," says the LORD. But you say, 'How have you loved us?' "Is not Esau Jacob's brother?" declares the LORD. "Yet I have loved Jacob but Esau I have hated. I have laid waste his hill country and left his heritage to jackals of the desert" (Malachi 1:2–3).

"And he will send out his angels with a loud trumpet call, and they will gather his elect from the four winds, from one end of heaven to the other" (Matthew 24:31).

"Then the King will say to those on his right, 'Come, you who are blessed by my Father, inherit the kingdom prepared for you from the foundation of the world'" (Matthew 25:34).

"And will not God give justice to his elect, who cry to him day and night? Will he delay long over them?" (Luke 18:7)

"'But there are some of you who do not believe.' (For Jesus knew from the beginning who those were who did not believe, and who it was who would betray him.) And he said, 'This is why I told you that no one can come to me unless it is granted him by the Father'" (John 6:64–65).

"I am not speaking of all of you; I know whom I have chosen. But the Scripture will be fulfilled, 'He who ate my bread has lifted his heel against me'" (John 13:18).

"You did not choose me, but I chose you and appointed you that you should go and bear fruit and that your fruit should abide, so that whatever you ask the Father in my name, he may give it to you" (John 15:16).

"But the Lord said to him, 'Go, for he is a chosen instrument of mine to carry my name before the Gentiles and kings and the children of Israel'" (Acts 9:15).

"Who shall bring any charge against God's elect? It is God who justifies" (Romans 8:33).

"So too at the present time there is a remnant, chosen by grace. But if it is by grace, it is no longer on the basis of works; otherwise grace would no longer be grace" (Romans 11:5–6).

"But when he who had set me apart before I was born, and who called me by his grace, was pleased to reveal his Son to me, in order that I might preach him among the Gentiles, I did not immediately consult with anyone" (Galatians 1:15–16).

"But we ought always to give thanks to God for you, brothers beloved by the Lord, because God chose you as the firstfruits to be saved, through sanctification by the Spirit and belief in the truth" (2 Thessalonians 2:13).

"According to the foreknowledge of God the Father, in the sanctification of the Spirit, for obedience to Jesus Christ and for sprinkling with his blood: May grace and peace be multiplied to you" (1 Peter 1:2).

"The beast that you saw was, and is not, and is about to rise from the bottomless pit and go to destruction. And the dwellers on earth whose names have not been written in the book of life from the foundation of the world will marvel to see the beast, because it was and is not and is to come" (Revelation 17:8).

3. I am indebted to my friend and colleague Timothy Beougher for bringing this point to my attention.

Chapter 11

1. Additional passages on God's holiness include the following: No one is holy like him (1 Samuel 2:2; Revelation 15:4). His name is holy (Psalm 105:3). His word is holy (Psalm 105:42). His temple is holy (Psalm 138:2). He is the Holy One of Israel (Isaiah 30:15). His Spirit is holy (Matthew 1:18). His city is holy (Matthew 4:5). Jesus is the Holy One of God (Mark 1:24). His Law is holy (Romans 7:12).

Chapter 12

1. Romans 9:18.

2. J. I. Packer, *Evangelism and the Sovereignty of God* (Downers Grove, IL: InterVarsity Press, 2008), 26.

3. Ibid., 30.

4. Additional passages on the universal nature of the invitation include the following:

"And it shall come to pass that everyone who calls on the name of the LORD shall be saved. For in Mount Zion and in Jerusalem there shall be those who escape, as the LORD has said, and among the survivors shall be those whom the LORD calls" (Joel 2:32).

"All things have been handed over to me by my Father, and no one knows the Son except the Father, and no one knows the Father except the Son and anyone to whom the Son chooses to reveal him. Come to me, all who labor and are heavy laden, and I will give you rest" (Matthew 11:25–28).

"For many are called, but few are chosen" (Matthew 22:1–14).

"And the master said to the servant, 'Go out to the highways and hedges and compel people to come in, that my house may be filled'" (Luke 14:21–23).

"He came as a witness, to bear witness about the light, that all might believe through him" (John 1:7).

"The true light, which enlightens everyone, was coming into the world" (John 1:9).

"For God so loved the world, that he gave his only Son, that whoever believes in him should not perish but have eternal life" (John 3:16).

"'All that the Father gives me will come to me, and whoever comes to me I will never cast out. . . . And this is the will of him who sent me, that I should lose nothing of all that he has given me, but raise it up on the last day. For this is the will of my Father, that everyone who looks on the Son and believes in him should have eternal life, and I will raise him up on the last day.' So the Jews grumbled about him, because he said, 'I am the bread that came down from heaven.' They said, 'Is not this Jesus, the son of Joseph, whose father and mother we know? How does he now say, "I have come down from heaven"?' Jesus answered them, 'Do not grumble among yourselves. No one can come to me unless the Father who sent me draws him. And I will raise him up on the last day. . . . It is the Spirit who gives life; the flesh is no help at all. The words that I have spoken to you are spirit and life. But there are some of you who do not believe.' (For Jesus knew from the beginning who those were who did not believe, and who it was who would betray him.) And he said, 'This is why I told you that no one can come to me unless it is granted him by the Father.' After this many of his disciples turned back and no longer walked with him. So Jesus said to the Twelve, 'Do you want to go away as well?' Simon Peter answered him, 'Lord, to whom shall we go? You have the words of eternal life'" (John 6:37, 39, 40–44, 63–68).

"On the last day of the feast, the great day, Jesus stood up and cried out, 'If anyone thirsts, let him come to me and drink'" (John 7:37).

"Truly, truly, I say to you, if anyone keeps my word, he will never see death" (John 8:51).

"And everyone who lives and believes in me shall never die. Do you believe this?" (John 11:26).

"Now when they heard this they were cut to the heart, and said to Peter and the rest of the apostles, 'Brothers, what shall we do?' And Peter said to them, 'Repent and be baptized every one of you in the name of Jesus Christ for the forgiveness of your sins, and you will receive the gift of the Holy Spirit. For the promise is for you and for your children and for all who are far off, everyone whom the Lord our God calls to himself'" (Acts 2:37–39).

"And it shall come to pass that everyone who calls upon the name of the Lord shall be saved" (Acts 2:21).

"Whoever confesses that Jesus is the Son of God, God abides in him, and he in God" (1 John 4:15).

"The Spirit and the Bride say, 'Come.' And let the one who hears say, 'Come.' And let the one who is thirsty come; let the one who desires take the water of life without price" (Revelation 22:17).

Chapter 13

1. While I was familiar with several of these perspectives, John Sanders listed others I had not yet encountered in *What About Those Who Have Never Heard? Three Views on the Destiny of the Unevangelized*, by Gabriel Fackre, Ronald H. Nash, and John Sanders (Downers Grove, IL: InterVarsity Press, 1995), 13–14. While I disagree with Sanders's conclusion regarding the destiny of those who never hear the gospel, his list is helpful in understanding the variety of perspectives today.

Chapter 14

1. While such is a rich tradition among some groups, there is absolutely no biblical support for infant baptism or for baptism endowing a person with saving grace (baptismal regeneration).

2. Based on this context, it is probably more likely that David simply was acknowledging that he would eventually go to the grave and be dead, like his child.

Chapter 15

1. Millard J. Erickson, *Christian Theology Today*, unabridged, one-volume edition (Grand Rapids, MI: Baker Book House, 1985), 846.

2. J. B. Lawrence, *The Holy Spirit in Missions*, 5th ed. (Atlanta, GA: Home Mission Board, 1966), 64.

3. John Stott, *Christian Mission in the Modern World*, 2nd ed. (Downers Grove, IL: InterVarsity Press, 1975, 2008), 186.

Chapter 27

1. I am indebted to my friend and colleague Dr. Paul Chitwood for this information. See "The Sinner's Prayer: An Historical and Theological Analysis" (Ph.D. dissertation, The Southern Baptist Theological Seminary), 2001.

Chapter 28

1. I actually said "follower of Isa" because the hairstylist was Muslim. *Isa* is the word used for *Jesus* in the Koran.

2. Ronald W. Johnson, *How Will They Hear If We Don't Listen? The Vital Role of Listening in Preaching and Personal Evangelism* (Nashville, TN: Broadman & Holman Publishers), 1994.

3. William Fay, *Share Jesus without Fear* (Nashville, TN: Broadman & Holman Publishers), 1999.

Chapter 31

1. Also in Acts, Luke recorded Peter's sermon to the household of Cornelius: "To him all the prophets bear witness that everyone who believes in him receives forgiveness of sins through his name" (Acts 10:43). In John's Gospel we also read, "But to all who did receive him, who believed in his name, he gave the right to become children of God" (John 1:12).

2. I recognize that after Peter's sermon on Pentecost, the Scriptures note: "Now when they heard this they were cut to the heart, and said to Peter and the rest of the apostles, 'Brothers, what shall we do?' And Peter said to them, 'Repent and be baptized every one of you in the name of Jesus Christ for the forgiveness of your sins, and you will receive the gift of the Holy Spirit'" (Acts 2:37–38). While some have taken this to support that the work of baptism brings salvation, such is not the case. Rather, the evidence that someone is following Jesus and has received the forgiveness of sins is that he will be baptized. Throughout the Bible and in Peter's future preaching (see Acts 10:43), salvation is by grace alone through faith alone.

Chapter 32

1. Here is an example of a tract that I often use: http://www.sbts.edu/documents/GRACE.pdf.

SOME BOOKS TO CONSIDER IN RELATION TO EVANGELISM

If you are interested in additional study on this topic, I have listed a few books to get you started that represent different perspectives.

General Evangelism

Drummond, Lewis A. *The Word of the Cross: A Contemporary Theology of Evangelism.* Nashville, TN: Broadman Press, 1992.

Johnson, Thomas P. *Charts for a Theology of Evangelism.* Nashville, TN: B & H Academic, 2007.

Reid, Alvin. *Evangelism Handbook: Biblical, Spiritual, Intentional, Missional.* Nashville, TN: B & H Academic, 2009.

Practical Books on Sharing Your Faith

Aldrich, Joseph C. *Life-Style Evangelism: Crossing Traditional Boundaries to Reach the Unbelieving World.* Portland, OR: Multnomah Press, 1981.

Barrs, Jerram. *Learning Evangelism from Jesus.* Wheaton, IL: Crossway Books, 2009.

Bright, Bill. *Witnessing without Fear: How to Share Your Faith with Confidence.* Nashville, TN: Thomas Nelson Publishers, 1993.

Coleman, Robert E. *The Master Plan of Evangelism.* 30th anniversary ed. Grand Rapids, MI: Fleming H. Revell, 1993.

_____. *The Master's Way of Personal Evangelism.* Wheaton, IL: Crossway Books, 1997.

Dever, Mark. *The Gospel and Personal Evangelism.* Wheaton, IL: Crossway Books, 2009.

Fay, William, with Linda Evans Shepherd. *Share Jesus Without Fear.* Nashville, TN: Broadman and Holman Pub., 1999.

Hybels, Bill and Mittelberg, Mark. *Becoming a Contagious Christian.* Grand Rapids, MI: Zondervan, 1996.

Hybels, Bill. *Just Walk across the Room: Simple Steps Pointing People to Faith.* Grand Rapids, MI: Zondervan, 2006.

Johnson, Ronald W. *How Will They Hear If We Don't Listen: The Vital Role of Listening in Preaching and Personal Evangelism.* Nashville, TN: Broadman and Holman Pub., 1994.

Kennedy, D. James. *Evangelism Explosion: Equipping Churches for Friendship, Evangelism, Discipleship, and Healthy Growth.* 4th ed. Wheaton, IL: Tyndale House Pub., 1970.

McCloskey, Mark. *Tell It Often—Tell It Well: Making the Most of Witnessing Opportunities.* San Bernardino, CA: Here's Life Pub., 1986.

McRaney Jr., Will. *The Art of Personal Evangelism: Sharing Jesus in a Changing Culture.* Nashville, TN: Broadman and Holman Pub., 2003.

Metzger, Will. *Tell the Truth: The Whole Gospel to the Whole Person by Whole People.* Downers Grove, IL: IVP Books, 2002.

Newman, Randy. *Questioning Evangelism: Engaging People's Hearts the Way Jesus Did.* Grand Rapids, MI: Kregel Pub., 2004.

Pippert, Rebecca Manley. *Out of the Saltshaker and into the World: Evangelism as a Way of Life.* Revised and expanded edition. Downers Grove, IL: InterVarsity Press, 1999.

Robinson, Darrell W. *People Sharing Jesus.* Nashville, TN: Thomas Nelson, 1995.

Spurgeon, C. H. *The Soul Winner.* New Kensington, PA: Whitaker House, 1995.

Thompson, W. Oscar Jr.. *Concentric Circles of Concern: From Self to Others through Life-Style Evangelism.* Nashville, TN: Broadman Press, 1981.

Wesleyan/Arminian Theology

Arminius, James. *The Works of James Arminius.* Lamp Post, Inc., 2009.

Finney, Charles. *Finney's Systematic Theology.* Abridged edition. J. H. Fairchild, editor. Minneapolis, MN: Bethany Fellowship, INC., 1976.

Pinnock, Clark H. *Grace of God and the Will of Man.* Minneapolis, MN: Bethany House Publishers, 1989.

Wesley, John. *The Works of John Wesley.* 3rd edition. Grand Rapids, MI: Baker Books, 2007.

Reformed/Calvinistic Theology

Calvin, John. *The Institutes of the Christian Religion.* Trans. Henry Beveridge. Peabody, MA: Hendrickson Publishers, 2008.

Packer, J. I. *Evangelism and the Sovereignty of God.* Downers Grove, IL: InterVarsity Press, 1961.

Sproul, R. C. *Grace Unknown: The Heart of Reformed Theology.* Grand Rapids, MI: Baker Books, 1997.

SCRIPTURE INDEX

5:16, 88
6:10, 78
7:1–5, 118
7:21, 88
9:35, 9
10:7, 7
10:16, 144
11:25–28, 164
11:27, 48
13:15, 162
18:1–6, 69
18:3, 162
18:8, 52
19:14, 69
22:1–14, 164
24:14, 9
24:31, 162
25:34, 162
25:41, 52
25:46, 52
28:19, 2, 7, 39, 86, 114, 148
28:20, 148

Mark
1:1
1:15, 161
1:24, 163
1:39, 89
2:24, 147
5:1–20, 95
5:7, 147
6:12, 161
9:43, 52
10:13–16, 69
10:21, 16
11:24, 79
13:11, 74
14:36, 99

Luke
1:16, 23, 162
4:14, 73
4:18, 1
5:27–32, 138
5:32, 161

7:50, 18
10:2, 79
13, 103
13:3, 60, 161
14:21–23, 164
15:7, 4
15:10, 99
16:23, 52
17:13, 125
18:1, 80
18:7, 162
18:13, 126
23:42, 126
24:46–49, 29
24:47, 86

John
1:7, 164
1:9, 164
1:12, 167
1:35–51, 138
3, 30, 95
3:3, 30
3:5–8, 26, 75
3:16, 10, 29, 53, 66, 122, 164
3:17, 54
3:19, 54
3:20, 54
3:35–36, 54
4, 95
4:34–38, 74
4:39, 138
5:40, 54
6:37–39, 44, 45
6:37, 39, 40–44, 63–68, 164
6:64–65, 162
7:37, 164
8:31–38, 59
8:51, 164
10:10, 10–11, 35, 134
10:27–29, 35
11:26, 164
12:12, 27
12:40, 162

13:18, 163
14:6, ii, 18, 62, 68
15:16, 163
16:8, 74, 102
17:2, 45
20:9, 27
20:21, 39

Acts
1:1–8, 73
1:8, 2, 39, 68, 86, 114
2:21, 165
2:37–39, 165, 167
2:38, 161
3:18, 10
3:19, 161–62
4:12, ii, 19, 62, 68
4:13, 74
4:20, 122
4:29–31, 74
6:10, 74
7, 102
8, 85
8:22, 161
8:26–38, 73
8:26–40, 89
9:15, 163
9:35, 162
10, 64, 89
10:1–8, 134
10:5, 64
10:42, 7
10:43, 10, 57, 167
10:44–48, 27
11:21, 22
13:48, 46–47
14:15, 10, 162
14:21, 7
15:3, 22
15:19, 162
16, 73
16:14, 75
16:30–32, 147
16:31, 126
17:11, 161
17:30, 161

GENERAL INDEX

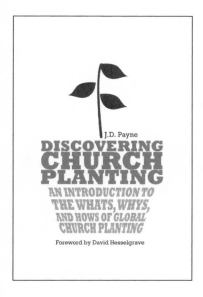

In *Discovering Church Planting*, J. D. Payne explores the biblical, historical, and missiological principles of global church planting as well as unfolding practical strategies for confronting contemporary challenges to our vital task in reaching a lost world. This comprehensive introduction to church planting shows the reader how to apply effective, international church planting practices to specific contexts. J. D. speaks from personal experience, research, and training and focuses on crucial issues every church planter should consider.

Paperback, 458 pages, 6 x 9
ISBN: 978-1-60657-029-6
Retail: $22.99

Available for purchase online or through your local bookstore.

ALSO AVAILABLE

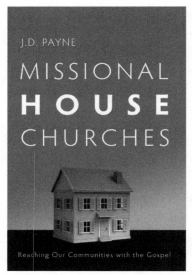

Missional House Churches examines the impact and effect that house churches are having in the United States in evangelizing, discipling, and church planting in local communities. Based on the author's firsthand research and interviews with over thirty missional house churches as well as his own experiences, this insightful work offers an inside look at and analysis of the workings of the missional house church.

This book will be of interest to students, church leaders, and mission-minded thinkers who wish to explore, understand, and participate in this growing phenomenon of the missional house church movement.

Paperback, 207 pages, 5.5 x 8.5
ISBN: 978-1-93406-825-0
Retail: $16.99

Available for purchase online or through your local bookstore.

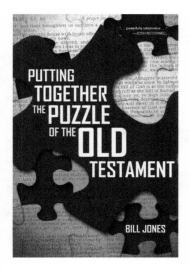

Intimidated! Overwhelmed! Totally confused! Descriptives such as these suggest how we often feel when it comes to the Old Testament. No wonder, with eight to nine hundred pages of names like Melchizedek, Mephibosheth, Meshelemiah, Michmethath, Mikhtam, who wouldn't feel this way?

If the Old Testament were one of those 1,000-piece puzzles, then this book provides the puzzle's box cover so you can understand the complete picture of what you are assembling. It also helps you put together the important four corners and all the straight-edged pieces so you have a completed border or frame of reference for the puzzle. Armed with these two advantages, when you read or study Old Testament stories, you will understand how all the pieces fit together.

This book is ideal for those who have little or no familiarity with the Old Testament or for pastors and lay leaders to help teach a better understanding of the Old Testament.

Paperback, 237 pages, 6 x 9
Retail: $16.99
ISBN: 978-1-93280-594-9

Available for purchase online or through your local bookstore.

ALSO AVAILABLE

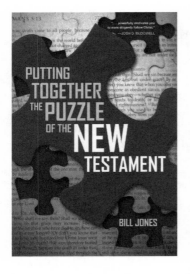

With hundreds of pages of stories, theology, and strange visions, sometimes the New Testament can be a bit confusing. How does it all fit together?

Imagine that the New Testament was a 1,000-piece puzzle. It's easier to figure out what you're putting together if you have the picture on the box to go by and the corners and straight edges as guides. The chapters in this book provide the puzzle's box cover, corners, and straight-edged pieces, demystifying the whole picture of what you are assembling. Armed with these advantages when you read or study New Testament passages, you will easily understand how the puzzle fits together.

This book pulls together the twenty-seven books of the New Testament into one compelling story, powerfully motivating you to more diligently follow Christ.
—Josh D. McDowell
Author of *Evidence That Demands a Verdict* and *More Than a Carpenter*

Paperback, 258 pages, 6 x 9
Retail: $16.99
ISBN: 978-1-60657-015-9

Available for purchase online or through your local bookstore.